THE
shark arm
Murders

Alex Castles

The thrilling true story of a Tiger shark
and a tattooed arm

Wakefield
Press

Wakefield Press
Box 2266
Kent Town
South Australia 5071

First published 1995
Reprinted 1995

Edited by Michael Bollen and Fiona Oates
Cover and book designed by Design BITE
Typeset by Clinton Ellicott, Adelaide
Printed and bound by Hyde Park Press, Adelaide

National Library of Australia
Cataloguing-in-publication entry

Castles, Alex C. (Alexander Cuthbert), 1933–   .
The shark arm murders.
ISBN 1 86254 335 6.

1. Murder – New South Wales – Sydney – Case studies.
I. Title

364.1523099441

Promotion of this book has been assisted by
the South Australian Government through the
Department for the Arts and Cultural Development.

Wakefield Press thanks Wirra Wirra Vineyards for its support.

The Shark Arm Murders

Alex Castles is an Emeritus Professor of
Law of the University of Adelaide, where
he taught for more than thirty years.
He is a law graduate of the Universities of
Melbourne and Chicago, a long time radio
and television broadcaster, the author or
co-author of eight other books on Australian
law and history as well as numerous other
publications in Australia, Britain, Canada
and the United States. He was formerly a
Commissioner of the Australian Law Reform
Commission and Research Fellow in the
United Nations Institute of Training and
Research in New York.

By the same author

Books

Introduction to Australian Legal History
Australia and the United Nations
Source Book of Australian Legal History
  (with J.M. Bennett)
Chronology of Australia
An Australian Legal History
Law on North Terrace
  (with A.L.C. Ligertwood and P. Kelly)
Law Makers and Wayward Whigs
  (with M.C. Harris)
*Annotated Bibliography of Australian Law,
  1788–1900*

Radio Series

New Law in an Old Land (with D. Connell)

To A.F.C., K.M.C. and D.O'D.,
who helped to rekindle my interest in
the Shark Arm murders.

AUTHOR'S NOTE

This book is a factually based account of two murders that happened in Sydney in 1935. For notes on my sources, please see the section at the back of the book.

Norval Ramsden Morris, criminologist and law teacher extraordinaire, first introduced me to the mysteries of the Shark Arm murders. A former New South Wales Police Commissioner generously gave me free access to all police archives dealing with these cases, and a former State Attorney-General provided copies of all the remaining transcripts of official hearings relating to them.

Two of my children, Kathryn and Alan, have been highly perceptive commentators and researchers in helping me prepare the manuscript in its final form. Other members of my family have graciously endured hearing of the events surrounding these crimes over a period of many years.

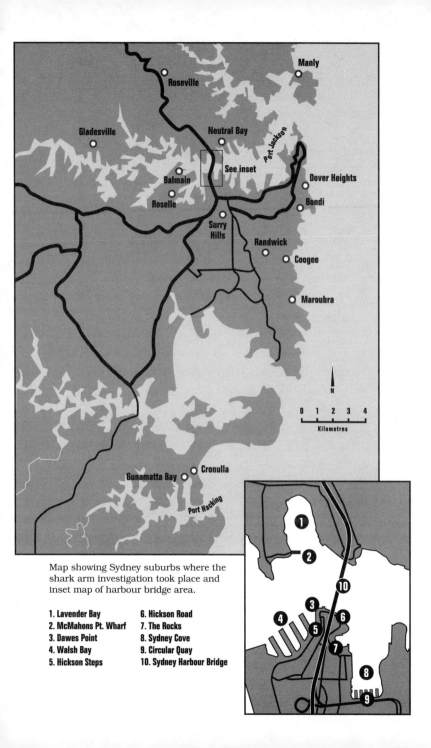

Map showing Sydney suburbs where the shark arm investigation took place and inset map of harbour bridge area.

1. Lavender Bay
2. McMahons Pt. Wharf
3. Dawes Point
4. Walsh Bay
5. Hickson Steps
6. Hickson Road
7. The Rocks
8. Sydney Cove
9. Circular Quay
10. Sydney Harbour Bridge

Contents

~~~~~~

Chapter 1

A PRIME TIGER SHARK

The morning of Sydney's Anzac Day in 1935 was autumn crisp and clear. More than 60,000 veterans marched through the city, watched by a crowd of over 300,000, nearly one third of the population of the metropolitan area. Before the march many old soldiers were at a dawn service and more than 250,000 people later attended a ceremony in open parkland near the city's downtown area.

After the national anthem was played to the solemn gathering, the day began to take on a different character. In contrast to Melbourne, Sydney's public entertainments were allowed to open for the remainder of the holiday. The picture houses along Pitt and George Streets announced that popular screen favourites of the moment were appearing, including Maurice Chevalier, Jeannette McDonald and Leslie Howard. Not far away, at the Tivoli vaudeville theatre, a new revue, 'Better Times', was doing good trade; people hoped that Australia's worst economic depression would soon be over. Rugby League fans made their way to the Sydney Cricket Ground, where Western Suburbs were playing St George.

Unusually, a large number of people planned to take the 'toast rack' trams to Coogee Beach, a rock-bound inlet on the Pacific Ocean, a few kilometres south of the entrance to Sydney Harbour. The area was normally deserted from autumn to spring, unlike during the summer months when visitors came in thousands to the seaside resort. The number of unseasonal visitors had grown rapidly during the past week, with especially large groups gathering over the Easter holiday weekend, which had ended a few days earlier.

Their destination was a building on Dolphin Street – variously known as the Coogee Baths or the Coogee Aquarium Baths – that had clearly seen better days. In 1887 it had been opened as one of the most luxurious entertainment centres in New South Wales, and had included a concert hall, a swimming pool, sideshows and eating places claimed to be among the best in the colony. Almost fifty years on, its paintwork was peeling and a distinctive, four-metre ironwork dome on its roof was rusting. The original seawater swimming pool – a poor imitation of Roman baths, decorated austerely with nineteenth-century plasterwork and columns – was all that remained in use.

On Anzac Day 1935, the visitors had not come to swim. For the past week the Coogee Baths had been the site of a much publicised exhibit. For perhaps the first time in the world, a large, live Tiger shark was on display. It had been captured eight days previously.

The shark was a prime specimen. Its maturity was confirmed by the dark-grey stripes that contrasted with the lighter grey of its body, the feature that gives these sharks their popular name. It was over four metres long and weighed about a tonne. Beneath the shark's blunt nose, its gaping jaws exposed sharp, serrated teeth.

On Anzac Day, visitors found the situation inside as

moribund as the crumbling edifice outside. The Tiger shark was mostly hiding moodily at the deep end of the twenty-five-metre pool, visible only as a slow-moving, almost amorphous grey mass. Many left quickly in disappointment.

For some Sydneysiders, Anzac Day was a normal working day. Detective-Constable Frank Head, an investigator with more than ten years in the state police service, was working quietly at his desk at the Randwick Police Station when he received a startling telephone message from Charlie Hobson, the proprietor of the Coogee Baths. It was brought by a constable who shouted out that Head would have to rush to Coogee as quickly as he could. A human arm was floating in the swimming pool.

At 5.45 pm, Head, accompanied by uniformed officer John Mannion, arrived at the Dolphin Street building. He expected to find himself confronted by a scene of carnage. Instead, he found Charlie Hobson and his brother Bert working calmly at the side of the pool, scooping fish bones and fins from the baths. Then he saw a whole left arm floating in the water at the shallower end of the pool. Clearly discernible, too, was a piece of rope attached to the wrist. Bert Hobson explained that he had used a stick to keep the arm close to the pool's edge, to prevent it from being eaten by the shark.

The detective set about recovering the arm from the water, deciding not to use a scoop or rake, which he feared might damage it. He knew that he had to act carefully, as the shark was moving up and down the pool, sometimes coming very close to the arm.

Head knelt at the side of the pool and, watching to ensure that the shark was at the far end, grabbed at the trailing rope. He satisfied himself that the rope was firmly attached to the limb, pulled it from the water in one quick movement, then lowered the arm gingerly onto an old hessian bag Charlie Hobson had placed beside him. A few seconds later, the huge shark cruised down the pool to where the arm had been floating. One snap of its jaws could have maimed Head for the rest of his life.

The detective, in his official report, noted: 'The arm is in a fair state of preservation except that the skin on the heel and palm of the hand has crumpled and become detached.' The rope attached to it, he wrote, was a piece of three-quarter-inch 'cheap manilla rope, tied around the wrist in a half-hitch knot'. He also reported on a variety of marks on the arm, describing two as 'large incised wounds' on the upper and lower parts of the limb. But his attention was mostly focused on a 'tattoo mark' on the 'inside forearm'.

The tattoo consisted of two tiny figures, about twenty centimetres high, facing up to each other in boxing gloves. It had been affected by its immersion in water – it was blurred in places – but its red and blue outlines were clear.

Having recovered the limb, Head was now charged with the responsibility of starting the search to discover where it came from. The tattoo was a potentially useful clue, but boxing was a popular sport in Sydney and the detective knew that there were probably many others like it. There was a chance that prints from the arm's fingers would enable an identification to be made, but only a remote one: Head was well aware that the police were only permitted to keep fingerprint records of people who had been charged with serious offences.

Like other detectives, Head had a good working knowledge of fingerprinting. As he studied the fingers and thumb, however, he recognised that he shouldn't risk taking impressions from them. They were puffy and drained of blood, too pliable to enable fingerprints to be recorded in the normal way. He left the pool area to telephone the fingerprint department of the Criminal Investigation Branch in downtown Sydney. An officer there warned him to keep everyone well away from the arm and said he would join him in less than an hour.

Meanwhile, Head set about questioning the Hobson brothers and the sprinkling of visitors who were still in the Dolphin Street building. Very quickly he found himself frustrated, troubled and confused. He could find no evidence to explain precisely how the tattooed arm had come to make its unheralded appearance in the Coogee pool.

Chapter 2

A LOST ARM

Detective Head learned from the Hobsons and their lingering customers that the calm of the Coogee pool's afternoon had been shattered just before 4.30 pm. The shark, which had seemed near death, had 'rapidly increased its pace' and repeatedly 'bumped against the side of the baths', causing loud echoes to ring from the high walls surrounding the pool area. Spectators had retreated from the edges of the pool. Some said that they had believed the shark was preparing to propel itself out of the water.

In the centre of the pool, the shark had turned 'rapidly in a sort of circle two or three times'. Its head, teeth exposed, had appeared above the surface of the water, then its splayed tail had sent water cascading into the air as it dived to the bottom of the pool. The frenzied commotion had ended as suddenly as it had begun, lasting no more than five minutes. Most of the spectators, it seemed, had been stunned by the incident. Several had cowered against the nearby walls. Amid the eerie silence which followed, the shark had 'resumed its normal manner of swimming again', as if nothing unusual had occurred.

Slowly, at first almost imperceptibly, the sensibilities of

those around the pool had been assailed again. A 'frightful smell' had lifted off the water, coming from an oil-like scum spreading out in the centre of the pool.

Charlie Hobson had been near the entrance to the pool on Dolphin Street at the time, preparing to close down for the night. He'd rushed inside when someone shouted out for him, fearing that his worst nightmare had come true, that a spectator had fallen into the pool with his man-eating exhibit. He'd been relieved to find that this wasn't so, but perturbed to see 'the water in the bath all dirty with grease'. He'd also noticed several objects floating in the water, and had asked his brother what had happened. Bert had explained that the shark had vomited uncontrollably.

Bert Hobson told Detective Head that, when the water had begun to clear, he'd recognised the remains of a rat and a bird. Then his attention had been drawn to a larger object floating by itself, about sixty-five centimetres long, with a piece of rope attached to it. After a second or two, he had realised that it was a human arm. The rat, he recalled, had been 'in a bad way' and had seemed to be 'partly digested'. The bird had been practically only feathers 'with hardly any meat' on it. The arm had looked to be in much better shape.

When Head began his questioning he faced no real difficulty. It seemed clear the arm had been regurgitated by the shark. One spectator said that he'd first noticed the arm when 'the shark was just underneath it, about two or three feet away'. The spectator agreed with Bert's observation that just before 'the water had been very clean and clear'. But Head, during two hours of intense questioning, grew puzzled on many fronts.

Firstly, when had the arm got into the shark? Impatiently

and disbelievingly, the detective questioned Bert Hobson over again about whether there had been any debris in the pool earlier on Anzac Day. Bert replied each time with a steadfast 'no'. He pointed out that he cleaned the pool regularly each morning. He had been on guard nearby for most of the afternoon, and he'd never once seen anything unusual in the pool.

For a moment Head thought he might have found an answer when he discovered that the water in the pool was changed several times a day, with fresh supplies brought in from the nearby ocean. But Charlie Hobson disabused him. The water entered a pipeline on the ocean floor. The pipeline was covered with a brass grating that weighed about 150 kilograms, making it very difficult to displace. The grating was finely meshed, with spaces of only about a quarter of an inch to allow the water to go through. Furthermore, even small objects could not pass through the electric pump that drew the water into the pool.

Nor could the detective get the Hobson brothers to agree that the arm could have been surreptitiously dropped in the pool. Bert pointed out he'd personally watched over the shark since its arrival, with only short breaks, from '7 am to 11 pm each day'. He'd stood guard, precisely to 'ensure that no spectators interfered with it'. Charlie insisted the pool area was secure from intrusions at other times. At night, the pool area was protected by roller shutters at the front of the premises. Charlie lived with his family in an adjoining flat in the same building, and someone there would have heard the noise of anyone attempting to break in.

Head was further nonplussed when the Hobsons claimed that the arm must have been inside the shark for at least seventy-two hours. Bert Hobson stated that 'it had not fed for three days previous' – the shark had refused to eat any of the fresh mackerel thrown to it at any time during this period. Quizzed again, Bert reiterated: 'It would not eat.' He also claimed that the shark had almost stopped moving, as if it might have been about to die, and that oxygen had been fed into the pool in a bid to revive it.

An exasperated Head jocularly suggested that next the brothers would be telling him the arm was already in the shark when it had been lodged in the pool, almost eight days previously. He was astonished when each seemed to agree, and even more confounded when Bert Hobson proceeded to explain how this was possible.

Disarmingly, Bert reminded Head of the remains of the rat and the bird. In the case of the rat, he was prepared to admit that it could have fallen into the pool after the shark's arrival there. But the bird was a different kettle of fish. The remains were those of a large sea bird, and neither of the Hobsons had any recollection of one like it being seen in the pool area, certainly not during the previous week. Bert was convinced that the bird had been snatched by the shark from the surface of the ocean well before it had been brought to the pool.

More compellingly, Bert referred Head to the pieces of a middle-sized shark he had recovered from the pool just before the detective had arrived. Some of the pieces were just bones. But others were bones with flesh. Bert was certain that these remains had already been in the shark, and explained why.

Bert, a fisherman, was the person who, with the help of a young nephew, had captured the shark alive and conveyed it to the pool. On the evening before it was caught, he'd placed a set line in the ocean off Coogee at a favourite spot.

He'd returned in the morning to find the Tiger shark thrashing around madly, its tail tangled inextricably in his line. It appeared to have been caught by accident while devouring a middle-sized shark that had already been hooked.

Bert believed it was the remains of this middle-sized shark that had been scooped from the pool. He told Head that, if any further proof was needed, he would swear unequi-vocally that no fish anywhere near the size of the smaller shark had been fed to the Tiger shark since its arrival at the Dolphin Street building.

The fisherman went on to advance another proposition that Head found just as intriguing. Bert reminded him that the remains of the rat and the bird were far more decomposed than the arm. Perhaps the arm had already been in the stomach of the middle-sized shark before that shark, in turn, had been partly eaten by the one he'd captured, thus protecting it from the Tiger shark's powerful digestive juices.

For Head, this was yet another conundrum. Just before midnight, he drove to the city to deposit the tattooed arm, wrapped loosely in the hessian bag that Charlie Hobson had provided, at the office of the Sydney Coroner. The Randwick detective hoped that the Coroner, who was responsible for leading inquiries into violent or unexplained deaths, would be able to find expert advice to help navigate the sea of riddles.

There was also some hope that the fingerprint branch might provide a beacon. During his visit to Coogee, Detective Head was briefly joined by a fingerprinting expert. Constable John Lindsay perceived at once that impressions could not be taken from the arm's fingers and thumb in the ordinary way, and set about a delicate operation which, to the best of his knowledge, had been attempted only once before in Australia and rarely overseas. The constable took a scalpel from his bag, cut at the skin around the thumb and fingers, prised it off with a pair of tweezers, and placed it in a special receptacle he had brought with him.

Head was heartened by Lindsay's belief that the operation had been carried out successfully. But the test, the fingerprint expert explained, would take place in the morning when the skin would be backed with padding, inked with great care, then pressed on an official recording card to see if the original minuscule lines on the surface of the fingers and thumb could be read accurately.

Chapter 3

MISMANAGED WEEKEND

On the Sunday after Anzac Day, three days after the tattooed arm had appeared in the Coogee pool, the Hobson brothers made a fateful decision. They decided that the Tiger shark was so badly ill that there was no purpose in keeping it alive, and killed it as humanely as they could with a harpoon-like spear. A fish oil merchant collected its remains from the Dolphin Street building the next morning. His only professional interest was to extract oil from its liver and sell it to a manufacturer who used it in medicinal preparations. 'I opened it up, took the liver for treatment and cleaned it out,' he reported to the police much later.

Neither the Coroner's office nor the police had told the Hobsons that the shark's body might be relevant to official inquiries. It disappeared, together with the contents of its stomach, into an anonymous mass of garbage on a rubbish dump, indistinguishable from other refuse. It was an ignominious end for a prince of the sea.

The police learned days later, when it was too late, that the fish merchant had opened up the shark's stomach and examined its contents. He hadn't carefully noted down what he had found. By the time he was questioned, he could only say that as best he could remember, he'd discovered more pieces of a middle-sized shark, some with flesh still adhering to them. He believed that there were no human bones, but admitted that he was not an expert on human anatomy. He was absolutely sure, however, that there had been no rope inside the shark like the piece attached to the arm in the Coogee pool.

With the disappearance of the shark's body, police would never know for sure whether there were more human remains to be found in the Tiger shark. Nor was it now possible to test Bert Hobson's speculation – that the tattooed arm had first been devoured by a middle-sized shark – by matching the Tiger shark's teeth with the markings on the arm.

Official misjudgements multiplied in the days that followed the discovery of the arm. They were brought about, in part, by the authorities' facile willingness to believe what they read in the newspapers.

Even while Detective Head was at Randwick typing a sober, accurate report, which would then make its way slowly through bureaucratic channels to CIB headquarters, the city's daily papers were preparing their own explanations of the events in the Coogee pool. Before Head arrived home, the morning *Daily Telegraph* had already reported that the arm was known to have once belonged to a person who had committed suicide by throwing himself into the ocean. The theory had one serious difficulty from the outset, in the shape of the rope that was firmly attached to the arm when it was found. The newspaper explained this away by declaring solemnly that it was 'known that suicides bind their wrists in this way', ignoring the absurdity that no one would be physically capable of tying their wrists together with half-hitch knots like the one Head had noted binding the manilla rope to the arm.

The presence of the knot made it more than likely that the arm had been tied to a heavy object before the attached body had been thrown in the sea. Head had already begun to suspect as much when he was at the Coogee pool, but it was a possibility that his colleagues in downtown Sydney simply ignored over the next three days. Instead, after another paper, the *Sydney Morning Herald*, provided much the same version of the suicide theory a day later, they instituted official inquiries on the basis that the arm had come from a suicide, seeking out files on people who had disappeared in recent weeks. The *Herald*, more highbrow than its morning contemporary, had suggested obtusely that the 'knots in the rope around the wrist were of the type a seaman would employ', as if that explained how a suicide might have tied them before plunging into the ocean.

The imaginings of the *Telegraph* and the *Herald* were more than matched by an article that was flashed around Australia from the offices of the *Sun*. This report suggested that the arm had found its way into the shark in the Coogee pool as a result of a prank by medical students. The arm had been spirited away from a dissection room at Sydney University, or stolen from a hospital after being amputated by a surgeon, then fed to the Tiger shark. Medical preserving fluid had protected the limb from the shark's digestive processes.

At the Coroner's office, this report was given far more credence than it deserved. Unlike some of his counterparts overseas, the Sydney Coroner had no medical or other scientific qualifications. He'd attained his position by long service in the hierarchical local court system. On the day after the arm's discovery, he called in two medical experts to view it. One was Dr Aubrey Palmer, the Government Medical Officer for the Sydney region, and chief adviser to the Coroner on the medical aspects of crime. The other was Dr Victor Coppleson, a surgeon who was not a forensic expert, but had a growing and well-deserved reputation for treating the victims of shark attacks. Despite these experts' presence, the Coroner himself was in charge of proceedings, and showed himself determined to hold on to the reins.

The viewing of the arm by the three men was little more than cursory. All were already very busy men, especially so during a week with two holidays. When they met they did not have the advantage of having Detective Head's report before them. Nevertheless, two months later, despite a further, more detailed examination of the arm by Palmer, the gathering on this occasion still provided the chief knowledge the Coroner had obtained about the arm.

The Coroner directed both Palmer and Coppleson to examine the top of the arm carefully to ascertain if it had been subjected to medical dissection. 'It was not done by a surgeon in an operation,' the Government Medical Officer proclaimed, and his medical colleague agreed. Each pointed out that a surgeon would have left flaps of skin at the top of the arm. Coppleson was equally sure the arm had not been bitten off by a shark. After a brief consultation, the experts decided that it had been cut off roughly 'by a sharp instrument at the shoulder joint'. But the Coroner was not completely satisfied that this disproved the prank theory. He had Palmer remove some tissue from the arm, with the aim of testing it for traces of preserving fluid.

The time spent on testing the *Sun*'s report seems to have left little for much else. The two gashes that Head had described as 'wounds' were not subjected to any close analysis. Coppleson guessed that they might have been from shark bites, but wasn't sure. Palmer thought they had probably been made by a sharp instrument like a knife, but wouldn't rule out the possibility that they had been made by glancing blows from bullets. Coppleson believed that other markings on the arm came from shark bites. Some of these were fainter and seemed smaller than others. In the absence of sufficient time to make a closer examination of them, he wasn't prepared to commit himself to the view that these fainter bites could have been made by a different shark.

Without the Tiger shark's body, the Hobsons' testimony or Head's report, the two medical experts could hardly confront the possibility that the arm was already inside the Tiger shark when it arrived at the Dolphin Street building. As best he could recall from the literature he had read on the subject, Coppleson thought it likely that the arm could only have been in the shark for forty-eight hours before its discovery. Palmer was prepared to argue it could have been longer, but without any scientific knowledge to support his view.

In contrast to the games at the Coroner's office, the fingerprint branch of the CIB acted with diligence and despatch. A preliminary microscopic examination showed that there were serious blemishes on parts of the arm's fingers and thumb. Constable Lindsay knew, however, that individual fingerprints are so unique that a good impression from even a single finger or thumb can make positive cross-identification possible. Nervously, he backed the wafer-like skin with padding, then cautiously inked its outside surfaces. Three fingers produced no more than messy smudges, but the minuscule lines on one finger and thumb appeared to be sufficiently intact to make legal identification possible, if matching prints could be found.

The result was a tribute to Lindsay's patient skill and the professionalism of the fingerprint branch. But the constable and his colleagues still faced the task of matching the fingerprints with the prints they were permitted to keep on file. There were many thousands of records to be inspected, and the officers began this time-consuming process, realising it might take many days, even weeks, before they exhausted every possibility.

Chapter 4

ROPE-MAKER

At about the same time, the editor of *Truth*, a popular Sunday newspaper, decided to publish an illustrated article about the discovery of the arm. He arranged for an artist to visit the Coroner's office to see it.

Truth was the only newspaper that many people in working-class suburbs purchased during the week. One of these readers was Edward Smith, a thirty-nine-year-old rope-maker, who lived in Newtown. He learned of the discovery of the arm for the first time when he read the paper on Sunday morning and saw the drawing the editor had commissioned. His attention was drawn to the article by the artist's depiction of the tattoo. He thought it could be the same as one on his brother's left arm.

Ted Smith's forty-five-year-old brother – known to his immediate family as Jim, although others mostly called him 'Jimmy' – hadn't been seen by his family for three weeks. Normally, the two brothers met once or twice a week to drink at local hotels. The rope-maker had checked at his brother's Gladesville home, and found that Jim hadn't been there either.

Ted Smith had discussed Jim's disappearance with Jim's wife, Gladys, but they had agreed not to report it to the police, at least for the time being. They knew that the missing man's activities sometimes took him away from home, and that they might involve matters he would not want the police to know about. But both were worried: it was unprecedented for Jim Smith to be absent for nearly a month without any contact at all.

Ted Smith took hours to make up his mind. He stared at the drawing in the newspaper again and again, deciding, in the end, that there could be little harm if he telephoned Frank Head, whose name had been mentioned in the newspaper article. Like most of the homes in the neighbourhood, Smith's had no private telephone, so he went to a public phone box nearby. When an officer from the Randwick Police Station came on the line, Ted nearly hung up and went home. He waited anxiously as the voice said he would try to find the detective.

After his name appeared in *Truth*, Head's colleagues at the Randwick Police Station teased him, claiming that he was basking in the glory. It was an accolade, they reminded him, that was not that easily won, particularly as the article in the paper rebounded to the credit of the police. In reality, Head was once more on rostered duty, trying as best he could to catch up on paperwork which, like other officers, he regarded as a bane. He took Edward Smith's call when it was transferred to him, and was impressed by Ted's obvious sincerity.

Head doubted whether the rope-maker could do much to assist in inquiries, but he was a great believer in personal contact and decided to visit Smith at his home. The paperwork could wait.

After a long conversation with Ted Smith, the detective

was still not convinced that the rope-maker knew anything that would help identify the person who had once worn the tattooed arm. But he was again impressed by Ted's obvious concern about the whereabouts of his brother. If only to allay Ted's fears, he agreed to arrange for the rope-maker and his sister-in-law to visit the headquarters of the Sydney CIB the next morning to examine photographs of the arm.

Head returned again to the piles of paper, as puzzled as ever by the case of the tattooed arm. Veteran detective that he was, Head suspected that Jim Smith had left home to avoid his obligations to his family. But he was also experienced enough to know that he could be wrong, and that chance might play a role in furthering investigations in any number of unexpected directions.

Chapter 5

THE BLACK BOOKS

There were congratulations all around in the fingerprint section of the Sydney CIB not long after 10 am on the Monday after Anzac Day. An officer found prints to match those taken from the skin that Constable Lindsay had collected at the Coogee pool. He reported that they were 'identical' and came from 'one and the same person'. No further proof was needed about who once shouldered the tattooed arm, but the identity could also be confirmed in another way. An official form accompanying the fingerprints listed some of the man's physical attributes. It mentioned the tattoo, describing it as boxers outlined in blue and red.

The matching of the prints happened soon after Ted and Gladys Smith finally managed to meet Detective Head in the headquarters of the CIB. The building was difficult to find, tucked away on a short thoroughfare called Central Street, more like an alleyway or a lane, that ran between George and Pitt Streets, not far from Sydney Town Hall.

The Smiths examined enlarged black-and-white photographs of the limb. Ted said: 'I have only seen a similar tattoo before that on my brother's arm.' Gladys was firm: 'The tattoo marks are the same as my husband had on his arm.'

Head conferred with the fingerprint branch in an adjoining room, and quickly discovered that Gladys was correct. Officers there found far more points of similarity between the two good impressions Lindsay had obtained and prints on file than the law required to make an identification conclusive. There were at least fifteen on one finger, and nineteen on the other. The fingerprint branch records showed that Jim Smith had been fingerprinted at Balmain on 12 September 1932, when he was charged with illegal gambling. They revealed that he had been convicted for this offence, the only conviction ever recorded against him.

Jim Smith, however, was far better known to the police at Central Street than this information suggested. Superintendent William Prior, the officer in charge of the Sydney CIB, pricked up his ears when he heard Smith's name, as did several of his colleagues. To all of them, Jim's solitary criminal conviction was no more than a minor peccadillo in a state where, in the absence of off-track wagering facilities, illegal betting was like an uncontrollable epidemic. Gambling convictions were widespread in New South Wales, particularly during the lead-up to the elections, when politicians would call for crackdowns in the name of law and order, before forgetting their noble sentiments until the next poll. What aroused Superintendent Prior's interest was rather the information about the missing man's activities that was to be found in the CIB's secret files.

Prior, at fifty-six and with thirty-four years in the state police, was at the zenith of his professional career. One colleague recalled: 'Bill Prior could sniff if there was a whiff of crime in the air.' To those who knew him best, however, Prior's success as a master detective and his appointment to one of the most prestigious law enforcement postings in Australia were based on a deeply inquisitive mind and a wealth of well-honed experience. Behind his back, his subordinates called him 'William the Silent' because of his taciturn ways with them: they attributed this to his country background.

The Superintendent's practical approach to his duties had helped to give him an encyclopaedic knowledge of the state's criminal milieu. He often brushed aside bureaucratic duties to spend hours out meeting his small army of informants scattered around Sydney: 'fizgigs' or 'fizzers' the police called them. He would receive cryptic notes from some, signed with numbers, rather than names, to hide the identities of the senders. In rare forthcoming moments, Prior told subordinates that 'a little bird on the shoulder whispering in the ear' was far more important in solving crimes than the cerebral processes of a Sherlock Holmes.

Prior had intervened in the inquiries even before he learned the arm had come from Jim Smith. On his return to Central Street after the weekend off, he'd castigated those who had blithely accepted that the arm was a suicide's. He suggested a far more sinister possibility – that a person's body had been weighted down and thrown into the sea in a bid to remove all traces of a murder.

This scenario grew clearer in the Superintendent's mind when he learned that the arm had been identified. He called for Head's report and noted that the detective had described two gashes on the arm as 'wounds'. A check with the Coroner's office revealed that the arm had been crudely amputated by a 'human agency'. Prior put two and two together and concluded that Jim Smith had died violently. He shook his head at the ineptitude of the Coroner, then called for several large dossiers to be brought to him from the CIB's records. He wanted to refresh his memory of police dealings with Jim Smith, expecting to find further confirmation that his instinct was sound.

In 1935, Superintendent Prior had none of the modern weapons of computer technology, forensic science or DNA profiling to help win the battle against crime. The dossiers he called for were a latter-day equivalent of the 'black books', a colloquial phrase that entered the Australian language in the first half of the nineteenth century, when it was used to describe records kept on British convicts in Van Diemen's Land and probably in New South Wales. These 'books' recorded not only convicts' official dealings with colonial authorities, but also other information about them, including the people they associated with and other activities they carried on.

The dossiers Prior summoned to his office were far more voluminous than those kept in colonial times. They were large manilla-backed collections of documents, mostly hand-written, including profiles of Jim Smith and others, records of official dealings with him in many guises, scraps of paper noting messages from fizgigs, and hurried, often poorly written notes from police officers. The work of a highly secret arm of the police service known as the Shadow Squad was also sometimes mentioned. This group of police officers worked undercover around Sydney, sometimes incognito for months and even years. Above all, the dossiers contained information on police inquiries into activities which extended well beyond a spot of illegal gambling.

Chapter 6

MAN ABOUT TOWN

In 1927 Jim Smith was noticed around Sydney and its suburbs in a fashionable new suit, which he wore with matching ties and highly polished shoes. At times he was seen wearing a tie-pin and cufflinks sprinkled with diamonds. His hair was carefully groomed, neatly parted and well slicked down in the manner of the period. To many of his neighbours in the working-class suburb where he lived he had become a 'man about town', hobnobbing with businessmen and drinking in the Marble Bar at Sydney's Hotel Australia.

But a dossier at the CIB revealed that Jim Smith's elegance was a charade. His clothes were paid for by someone else, the diamond ornaments rented by the day from a pawnbroker. Smith was holding himself out as a building contractor, without any previous experience in the trade.

Superintendent Prior carefully noted this time as a watershed in Jim Smith's life. Following his arrival in Australia before the first world war as an immigrant just out of his teens, Jim Smith spent his time before 1927 in inner-city working-class suburbs around Balmain. He made his home there, married Gladys Molloy who lived there, and his only child, Raymond, was born in the neighbourhood. The area was a place of reasonable opportunity compared to the way of life his family had endured in the north of England. Jim adapted himself well to his new environment, soon losing his north-country accent, developing new and sometimes enduring friendships, and relishing the camaraderie he found in hotel bars and billiard saloons.

But he was more adventurous and ambitious than most of his acquaintances, despite the limited education he had received in England. He sailed to Australia alone before the other members of his family, and soon after embarked on a career as a professional boxer. It was one of the few occupations where those with limited education or training might rapidly improve their station. The tattoo on his left arm was a memento of his boxing days.

Physically, Jim Smith had many of a boxer's attributes. He was square-jawed, hard-headed, lean and tough, of medium height and weight. He was also tenacious, and trained obsessively. He began his professional career at a place called Hatty's Arcade, a makeshift boxing establishment in a local shopping centre, and enjoyed fleeting moments of glory at a theatre called the Gaiety, near Central Railway Station, where boxing competed with vaudeville performances. Finally, he was engaged for preliminary bouts at the Newtown Stadium, for many years one of Sydney's two main boxing venues. In top company, however, he was soon found wanting. Despite his strength of purpose, he lacked the natural reflexes and the mental tuning necessary to become a champion professional boxer.

To Superintendent Prior and colleagues, Smith's career as a boxer exemplified far more than a year or two spent entering a canvas ring. It also helped to point them in the direction of what might have happened to him almost a generation later. After several bruising defeats, Smith showed no real capacity to understand when situations might be moving beyond his control. Optimistically, ultimately recklessly, he ignored the signs that his hopes of making it to the big time were beyond him. His brother and other members of his family had to battle with his anger and resentment before he gave the game away.

After Smith stopped boxing he moved from one casual job to another, seemingly with little purpose in life, until he obtained regular work as a barman in a Balmain hotel. It was hardly a top job – he was also employed to act as the 'chucker out', as the local idiom described a person who removed unruly customers from the premises. But, according to regulars, after a while his old optimism revived. He began to tell stories of his days in the ring, embellishing them with gusto. He boasted of his acquaintance with the 'immortal' Les Darcy, the greatest Australian prize-fighter of the period, who had fought many of his most famous bouts at the Newtown Stadium.

Police dossiers confirmed that up to this time Jim Smith had distanced himself from the neighbourhood's criminal activities. As a young man, he refused to join any of the local 'pushes' – gangs that roamed the inner suburbs of several Australian state capitals at the time, including Sydney. Unlike the hero in C.J. Dennis's poem 'The Sentimental Bloke', Smith was never known for 'stoushing johns' – brawling with the police. He also avoided the more vicious street gangs that terrorised their victims, including local businessmen, with sharpened razors and knives during the years immediately after the first world war.

But Jim Smith's blameless life began to change, and the police records touching on his activities started to expand rapidly, after he left the Balmain hotel to take up a new occupation. His new job was in the billiard room of a city men's club called Tattersalls. From the outset, it gave him a veneer of respectability he seemed to relish. At the Balmain hotel he'd often served behind its bar in a flannel singlet and trousers. But at Tattersalls he was required to dress neatly in a suit and tie with a well-ironed shirt. His job was to keep the billiard tables in good order and do other maintenance work. He also acted as a 'marker', recording players' scores on boards attached to the wood-panelled walls of the billiard room. In this capacity he mingled with the clientele, helping to settle disputes, and ingratiating himself with the regulars by handing them favourite cues without being asked. He soon found that the billiard room was not always what it seemed – it was a venue where 'deals' were made. Some that he overheard were everyday business transactions, but others were clearly of dubious legality.

These discussions reflected the character of the club's membership, which largely consisted of men associated with racing and gambling, including owners of thoroughbred racehorses, bookmakers and some of the biggest punters in Australia. A number had connections with the large, illicit betting industry that flourished around the country. Others had long been high-rollers in the illegal gambling carried on at secret inner-city locations.

Jim Smith was fascinated by the way many of the activities discussed in the billiard room were carried on with impunity, despite their patent illegality. He listened attentively as his clients boasted of their 'arrangements' with politicians and police. Crime, it seemed to Jim, operated on two sides of a divide, as wide as the social gulf that separated Balmain from Sydney's upper-class neighbourhoods. Some of his neighbours at home were regularly sent to gaol for minor offences; some even for consorting with their friends. At places like Vaucluse and McMahon's Point, on the other hand, some people appeared to carry on criminal activities with little or no risk to themselves.

The first indication that this knowledge affected Jim Smith's planning for his future came to the police when he left to become 'proprietor' of a billiard saloon at Rozelle that was backed by members of the Tattersalls club. It was a seedy establishment, located in an old-fashioned shop in a run-down shopping area not far from Balmain. By day it catered for a local clientele – billiards, snooker and cards. But at night, contemporary police reports disclosed, the business became a gambling den. Well-dressed men left expensive limousines parked outside for many hours.

Despite regular surveillance by the police, no official action was taken to stop the illicit gambling. Official reports made no mention of the politicians and other prominent citizens who had been there at night. Jim Smith recognised that, with the backing of men with money and official connections, he had made a change for the better in his life.

At Rozelle, however, he was little more than a 'front' for his wealthy backers, making only small profits for himself. Suddenly, after three years, and with the blessing of those who had backed him in the enterprise, he gave up the proprietorship of the billiard saloon. It was, police records suggested, the most fateful move of his life, although Smith had no cause to realise it at the time.

Almost overnight, at the suggestion of a professional man who'd been a gambler at his Rozelle premises, Jim Smith entered the building trade. With no previous experience at all, he emerged as a master builder with a handsome contract to erect fourteen flats on a vacant lot in the prestigious suburb of McMahon's Point, just across the harbour from central Sydney. The lot belonged to a North Sydney boatbuilder named Reginald William Lloyd Holmes, who lived with his family nearby. He was known for his seemingly impeccable business connections.

Within days of giving up the Rozelle business, Smith was getting about in new, flashy attire. Despite the weight he was gaining as he approached middle age, he cut a dashing figure as he did the rounds of building suppliers and sought extended credit to obtain the materials to build the flats. His 'word was his bond', he told suppliers, promising that they would be paid in full when the work was completed. Many – glancing at his clothes and the diamonds he sported, and remembering that the flats were being erected for Reginald Holmes – believed him. They soon discovered their error.

As Superintendent Prior continued to delve into the CIB files, he became increasingly convinced that Jim Smith's entry into the building trade had been a dangerous mistake, and that what had followed in its wake could well explain the boxer's premature demise.

Chapter 7

A TOUCH OF BLACKMAIL

'When thieves fall out there can be hell to pay.' The updated version of an ancient saying intruded on the Superintendent's thinking as he examined police documents on the relationship between Jim Smith and Reginald Holmes. There was nothing to prove that animosity between them had brought about the missing man's disappearance. But there were pointers to the probability, with blackmail by Jim Smith a likely root cause.

The relationship between Smith and Holmes was a classical situation where blackmail could occur. The boatbuilder was highly vulnerable if his dealings with Smith were ever revealed, even if only by way of rumour. To all appearances, Holmes was a pillar of respectability. He was in charge of a long established family business on the shoreline of Lavender Bay, alongside the northern approaches to the Sydney Harbour Bridge. Aged forty-three in 1935, married with two children, he was almost, but not quite, an accepted member of Sydney high society. He dined at the Royal Sydney Yacht Club, and was noted for his support of his local Presbyterian Church. Tall, lean and sun-bronzed, he was an expert yachtsman and speedboat driver, who exuded confidence in meetings with 'inferiors' like Jim Smith.

Smith's capacity to blackmail Holmes went back to the building of the flats at McMahon's Point. They were erected in the Lavender Bay street in which the boatbuilder had his residence and business establishment. The police files suggested that Holmes was the main beneficiary of an elaborate scheme to cheat the building suppliers who gave Smith extended credit. The scheme enabled the flats to be obtained for much less than they were really worth. A maze of legal documentation recorded that Smith was paid in full for his work, which should have enabled him to meet the claims of the suppliers. In reality, if the police suppositions were correct, Smith was paid much less for his services, and was never given the money to pay creditors. Smith was declared bankrupt, with no worthwhile assets to his name. The owner of the flats legally had no responsibility for the debts, the suppliers received nothing, and Holmes and his conspirators made a large profit.

Until his discharge from bankruptcy, Smith was paid in secret instalments by the entrepreneurs of the building scheme, enabling him to live in reasonable comfort without working while ensuring that no money would be available to his creditors. During his bankruptcy, Smith's most gainful occupation was in the betting rings at Randwick and Rosehill race-courses, where he flaunted his acquaintance with leading bookmakers and others he'd met at the Tattersalls club. In between race meetings he spent much of his time in hotel bars or billiard saloons. He clearly enjoyed his gregarious existence. After his discharge from bankruptcy, however, no further money was owed to him under the original arrangement, and Smith needed a large sum for a new business venture. It was at this juncture, police surmised, that he probably blackmailed

Holmes for the first time, threatening to expose the boat-builder to the police for his role in the building of the flats.

Whether the result of blackmail or not, Smith found himself the proprietor of a new business, backed by three hundred pounds from Reginald Holmes, a large sum given that the ordinary wage in Sydney was less than five pounds a week. Smith's new venture – the Rozelle Athletic Club – sounded grand, but it was another ordinary billiard saloon, with ancient tables scattered around.

Police information suggested that Holmes's payment was intended as a final discharge of obligations to Jim Smith. But Superintendent Prior knew that blackmailers frequently hoodwink victims by telling them that one payment, or the granting of a particular favour, is all that is needed and there will be no more threats.

Jim Smith's new venture was a disaster for him. He overlooked, or simply ignored, that he no longer had the patronage of the Tattersalls club members who had backed and protected him before. Once again, his reckless optimism betrayed him. In September 1932 he was fingerprinted at the Balmain Police Station and convicted for allowing illegal betting at his newly acquired Rozelle saloon. The fine had been troublesome enough, but the conviction was a more serious blow. His registration as a billiard saloon proprietor was cancelled and he had to give up the Rozelle business with hardly any financial compensation.

Smith found himself cut adrift from his old world, in which illusion had obscured reality. He drifted along for three years and more. Suddenly, in the midst of a great economic depression, he had no regular financial support. The Smiths' rent was sometimes unpaid, welfare assistance was hardly enough to sustain his family, and there seemed to be no opportunities for employment.

Then, without any obvious explanation, Smith's situation changed dramatically. By early 1934 he had moved his family away from the tenement-lined streets of inner-Sydney to Gladesville, on the other side of Sydney Harbour, a step upwards on the social scale, if only a short one. The Smiths had far more living space around them at their new Batemans Road home, and even the makings of a front garden.

Jim Smith's spirits rose, and so, it seemed, did his fortunes. More than one police officer noted him single handedly sailing large yachts around Sydney Harbour and into the open sea, normally only the prerogative of the very rich and their associates. An officer at Balmain was astounded to see Smith at the wheel of one of the most expensive and powerful speedboats in Australia. The former boxer took to wearing a peaked seaman's cap, and the children who lived near his new Gladesville residence called him 'skipper'. Jim responded by raising his right hand to his cap, addressing them with a smart naval-style salute.

Well into middle age, and with the same dedication he had shown in his boxing career, Jim Smith transformed himself in a few months into a highly competent seaman. His old drinking companions at Balmain were astounded by the change, and mystified when he brushed away their questions with a nod or a wink. But the police were not so confused. As one of the fattest dossiers given to Prior revealed, Jim Smith's seafaring was the result of a renewed association with Reginald Holmes. It appeared Jim probably blackmailed the boatbuilder into employing him soon after he was forced to abandon the Rozelle Athletic Club.

Police documents indicated that, however their new collaboration came about, the two men appeared to work quite amicably with each other for a time. But there was evidence that they were soon trading insults and threats.

To many people who met and dealt with Holmes, it would have seemed beyond belief that he was no stranger to violence, kept a loaded pistol in his office desk, and might have schemed to do away with Jim Smith. But not many people were privy, as Superintendent Prior was, to evidence in the secret files of the CIB.

The building of the flats had provided only a glimpse of the cultivated boatbuilder's crooked side. It was most clearly revealed by his involvement in waterfront crime over many years. A police officer once reported to Prior that among Holmes's long-term associates was a waterfront criminal known as 'Gravy Eyes'. Other, less official informants, whom Prior knew by names like 'Captain Seaweed' and 'Seaweed', provided details of Holmes's criminal activities, as did the members of the police Shadow Squad whose beat included hotels, such as the First and Last Hotel on Circular Quay, where waterfront criminals congregated.

Holmes's chief criminal activity on the waterfront was smuggling. Whereas some smugglers lifted goods off overseas ships at the docks, the boatbuilder preferred a more adventurous, but generally safer method, which was difficult to control. 'Agents' in overseas vessels would throw contraband into the open sea at pre-arranged locations. Men in speedboats capable of outstripping the slower boats used by the police and customs officers would collect the contraband, and land it at secluded locations on Sydney Harbour or on the coast nearby. If it seemed a smuggler's vessel was about to be apprehended, consignments would be dumped overboard, making it difficult for law enforcement agencies to produce evidence enough to sustain convictions.

Smuggling was a lucrative trade. One of the favourite imports was cocaine, used mostly by the members of the 'younger set', as newspapers described junior members of Sydney's upper-class society. Even by later standards, the value of some consignments was extremely high. One, dumped overboard in 1935 off Wollongong, south of Sydney, was recorded as being worth five thousand pounds, more than one hundred thousand dollars half a century later. Police records of the time referred to other hauls of similar value.

A smuggler's life was not for the faint-hearted. The financial stakes were high, and opposing syndicates battled for business, particularly in the narcotics trade. At times open warfare almost broke out, and Holmes was often implicated.

Documents in front of Superintendent Prior stated that the boatbuilder carried a pistol when confronting his rivals. One report said that Holmes's smuggling syndicate intended to 'kidnap' the leader of a rival gang because 'he had been doing them a lot of harm with the smuggling'. Another claimed the boatbuilder intended to have the same man 'bumped off'. An incident relating to the same dispute was corroborated for the police by information gathered from three separate sources. Holmes lured one of his main competitors in the smuggling trade on to a vessel anchored in Sydney Harbour. At their meeting the boatbuilder grew angry when his rival refused to collaborate with him. The man himself later recalled that Holmes then 'took a revolver from his pocket and shot three shots into the water', with the clear implication that next time the pistol would be aimed at him if he didn't accede to the boatbuilder's demands.

With this background knowledge, it took no leap of faith for Prior to conclude that Holmes might well be involved in Jim Smith's disappearance, whatever the boatbuilder's compatriots at the Royal Sydney Yacht Club and his local Presbyterian Church thought about him. And Prior had more documents to bolster his suspicion. They related to the sinking of a yacht called the *Pathfinder*.

Chapter 8

A LAST VOYAGE

The *Pathfinder* was a sturdy luxury yacht that once traversed Sydney Harbour and the ocean beyond with grace and speed. In April 1934, it sank in deep water off Terrigal, then a small town just north of Sydney. The vessel disappeared in a turbulent sea on an overcast morning. Visibility was impeded by frequent squalls passing across the area.

The sinking of the yacht attracted public attention. The yacht was well-known and, despite its age, was insured for a sum worth a hundred and fifty thousand dollars today.

The police records showed that the sinking of the luxury yacht was part of a scheme, involving Reginald Holmes and several associates, to defraud marine insurance companies on a grand scale. According to this plot, the conspirators would transfer vessels like the *Pathfinder* to 'dummy' owners at grossly inflated values. They would cover their tracks with intricate legal documentation, in which it would appear that the full purchase price had been paid by the new 'owners'. In fact no purchase money would change hands at all, and the vessels would remain in the hands of their original owners. The boats would then be valued at inflated prices for insurance purposes, with 'experts' like Holmes standing by to help convince insurance company representatives of their purported value. After a discreet interval, the boats would be 'accidentally' lost at sea and the conspirators would collect the insurance, sharing the difference between the real value of the vessels and the amounts paid for their loss by insurers.

Holmes and his associates tested the scheme in 1933 in a cautious 'practice exercise' with a small yacht. After all of the agreed procedures were carried out, the vessel was set alight off the south coast of New South Wales, and disappeared without a trace. The conspirators made a modest profit after the boat's dummy owner claimed the insurance.

Holmes and his cronies were emboldened by this success. They planned for the sinking of the *Pathfinder* to be the first of many occasions when the scheme would bring them far larger profits. After the preliminaries were completed and the vessel was transferred to its bogus owner – a real estate agent named Gregory Vaughan – the conspirators succeeded in having the *Pathfinder* over-valued for insurance. It was then sailed to a mooring on the Hawkesbury River estuary north of Sydney, loaded down with rocks in the dead of night, and left for several weeks. On a day when bad weather was forecast, the *Pathfinder* was sailed out into the open sea on its planned last voyage.

The scheme began to fall apart, however, when the deck officer on a collier heading south from Newcastle noticed the foundering yacht and diverted his vessel to go to its assistance. As he approached the *Pathfinder*, he saw a lone man rowing away in a small dinghy. He was making little headway against the boisterous weather. The officer shouted to him through a megaphone offering to take him on board, but was amazed to see the oarsman brush the air with one hand in a quick dismissive wave.

The officer reluctantly ordered the collier to resume its original course, and noted the incident in its log. He turned back several times, watching the yacht sinking gradually beneath the water. Through his binoculars he saw the lone oarsman battling against a heavy swell towards the shore several kilometres away. The officer later reported the incident to the police, telling them that he suspected the yacht was deliberately scuttled.

Two hours after the collier sailed away from the *Pathfinder*, the lone oarsman beached near Terrigal. Spray-swept and soaked to the skin, he arrived at the local police station, identified himself as Jim Smith, and blurted out to the officer on duty that the yacht had sprung a leak in the rough weather and sunk. He repeated his graphic story on the telephone a few minutes later, telling the officer who made the connection for him that he was ringing the owner of the yacht, Reginald Holmes.

In the normal course, Smith's request to speak to Holmes would have gone unnoticed. By the time the report from Terrigal was received by the Sydney CIB, however, officers had ascertained that the legal owner of the *Pathfinder* was the real estate agent Gregory Vaughan, who had already denied any everyday connection with Holmes. A conscientious officer at Central Street double-checked with the Terrigal police. The officer there had no doubt that Jim Smith had asked to be connected to Reginald Holmes, and that Smith had said that Holmes was the *Pathfinder*'s owner. The officer told his colleague that he not only remembered clearly the name of the man Smith was calling, but had even spoken to him momentarily when he'd made the connection.

The police investigation that followed was painstaking and thorough until slowly, but inexorably, Holmes and his associates became aware that they were faced with an unpalatable choice. If they wished, they could claim the insurance money. But, police let on, they would then be charged with criminal offences that carried long gaol sentences. They finally realised they had no real choice at all, and gave up hope of pursuing any insurance claim. Holmes and his confederates lost a valuable yacht without any financial compensation and incurred a host of other expenses.

In the bitter recriminations that followed, Holmes in particular singled out Jim Smith as the principal architect of the debacle. He lambasted him for his recklessness, and peremptorily severed his connections with the former boxer.

Jim Smith was left desperate, having to borrow money from his brother Ted to help sustain his family. He believed Holmes had cheated him out of the five hundred pounds he had been promised to sink the *Pathfinder*. As some of Holmes's employees later reported to the police, Smith appeared at the Lavender Bay boatyard, openly haranguing the boatbuilder and calling him a traitor. He called at the boatbuilder's home, sometimes accompanied by his wife, demanding to see his erstwhile patron, telling Holmes's wife that her husband owed him money.

One of Holmes's associates paid Smith one hundred and fifty pounds in a bid to placate him. When the boatbuilder heard of it he reacted angrily, telling his crony that Smith was a 'blackmailing bastard' who would only return for more if he wasn't 'put out of the way'.

In all of this, there was no evidence proving that Reginald Holmes was responsible for Jim Smith's disappearance. For Superintendent Prior, however, it was a further indication that the boatbuilder had reason to silence his former employee. Unhesitatingly, the Superintendent decided that the relationship between Smith and Holmes had to be given top priority in the police inquiries.

Chapter 9

A SECRET LIFE

Superintendent Prior, and very few others, had access to a document that revealed the most highly guarded secret of Jim Smith's life. It was written in official police jargon, but still evoked the grave dangers the missing man had faced over the last three years.

The document told how, in the second half of 1932, a police sergeant made his way inconspicuously to a jetty at Long Nose Point, a promontory at the northern end of the Balmain peninsula. It was mid-morning on an ordinary working day and he was pleased to see that no one else was around. But as minutes passed, he grew annoyed when a man he was supposed to meet at 10 am did not appear.

The sergeant, surnamed Arantz, decided to wait a little longer, and tramped on to the jetty, where he was startled to hear a muffled voice calling out from nowhere, 'Get Aboard.' He wondered what was happening until an engine roared loudly beneath him and a launch appeared beside the jetty, Jim Smith at the helm. Arantz's report continued: 'I got into the launch and he pulled it out into the stream and stopped the engine.' Out of earshot from land, the pair were soon deep in conversation. Smith told the sergeant about some of his activities with Holmes.

Meetings between the two men had begun not long before. Their rendezvous at Long Nose Point was typically furtive. Both knew that Jim Smith faced serious threats to his life if his associates learned that he had become a police fizgig.

Jim Smith lived with his family in a milieu where 'dobbing in a mate' was a cardinal sin, more reprehensible even than providing 'scab' labour to break a union strike. Dobbing was rewarded with social ostracism. Suspected informers would find no one to drink with in a hotel bar, their families would be denied service in local shops, and children harassed at school.

Jim Smith understood all this, and feared it. But he was given no real choice. In time-honoured fashion used by law enforcement agencies around the world, Arantz enticed him into the job.

The association between the two men began when Smith was destitute and desperate to support his family after giving up the Rozelle Athletic Club. The police record of Smith's recruitment stated: 'Detective-Sergeant Arantz interviewed Smith regarding the theft of a number of billiard and snooker balls.' It then revealed that no charges had been brought. Blandly, it disclosed that the allegedly stolen items had been 'returned'. For this police indulgence, the would-be businessman agreed to become a police informer.

Unbeknown to Smith, he was carefully targeted. During his halcyon years, when he lived on the ill-gotten proceeds from the flats at McMahon's Point, he developed friendships among what newspapers described as the 'criminal class'. Some of these friendships had grown stronger, and their range had expanded, during his time as the proprietor of the Rozelle Athletic Club.

Smith was expected to report on the activities of some of the most dangerous, volatile criminals in Sydney – tough, hardened men, many with long prison records. His most perilous task was to provide information on 'graduates' of the razor gangs that had terrorised parts of inner Sydney immediately after the first world war. This group included well-known gunmen, as well as men who still carried the sharpened razors and knives that had made them notorious as they forced businesses to buy protection. Some carried scars as mementoes of street gang battles. A few were so prone to violence that they attacked each other over imagined insults or arguments about the turn of a card. Almost without exception they reserved their most violent reactions for anyone suspected of collaborating with the police.

From the beginning of their association, Arantz knew about the risks Jim Smith faced. A faint suspicion, even a malicious rumour, that he was a 'crab', a 'shelfer' or a 'dropper man', as fizgigs were also described, would have seriously threatened Smith's wellbeing, perhaps even his life.

Sergeant Arantz took great pains not to reveal Smith's identity as a fizgig, even in conversations with his fellow officers. But there were occasions when Jim Smith gave him warning of crimes that would involve gunmen in banks and other places where ordinary people could get hurt. After careful deliberation and conversations with Superintendent Prior, Arantz passed on this intelligence to several officers who were given orders to catch the gunmen in the act before they could do any harm.

In one case, Jim Smith's information was instrumental

in the apprehension of two men attempting to defraud a bank. In another, an armed hold-up was forestalled. Prior and Arantz believed that the use of Smith's intelligence in these circumstances was well justified, but both were left concerned about his safety. The two men caught in the bank fraud – Messrs Cottenham and Weyman – were tried and convicted, with Cottenham serving a prison term. Prior's informers told him that the men believed Jim Smith had 'shelved' them, and had sworn vengeance. Arantz confirmed to Prior that there were other dangerous criminals who believed that Smith had dobbed them in.

In Jim Smith's secret life as a fizgig, Superintendent Prior discovered another reason to suppose the boxer might have died violently.

Chapter 10

A TALL ORDER

The Sydney CIB in 1935 had antecedents dating back to the first half of the nineteenth century. By tradition, and measured by its successes in the intervening years, it was the local equivalent of England's Scotland Yard or the French Surete. But it faced one of the most daunting tasks ever when Superintendent Prior decided to launch a full-scale investigation into the disappearance of Jim Smith.

Legally there was no proof that the missing man was dead. Informants reported street rumours that he was still alive. The experts who had examined the tattooed limb at the Coroner's office believed Jim Smith could not have survived the crude amputation, but were not prepared to state this categorically.

The last time any of the missing man's family had seen him alive was seventeen days before his arm had made its unlikely appearance in the Coogee pool. No one seemed to know what might have happened to him in the interim, and no one was clear about precisely when his arm had been swallowed by the Tiger shark. Significantly, neither of the experts who viewed the arm at the Coroner's office were prepared to concede it had been in the shark when it was captured in the open sea.

The Superintendent did not disdain the advice of medical and other experts. But he was aware of their professional conservatism – their unwillingness to venture towards the unknown – even when the available facts might point in this direction. Prior had a far more open mind. Unlike the medical experts, for instance, he wouldn't discount the possibility that the arm had been inside the Tiger shark before it reached the Coogee pool. He had no illusions about the formidable job the police faced, but, in his own pragmatic way, he believed that the information he had at his disposal gave the investigation something to work with.

Prior's Central Street subordinates knew that whenever the Superintendent summoned two of his most experienced officers, the CIB was on the verge of a major, difficult investigation. Ordinarily, only one man was placed in charge of an inquiry. This time, however, Prior was preparing to establish what in later times would be described as a task force, a team of officers led by two men with other detectives to assist them.

With only one indisputable piece of evidence to go on – the tattooed left arm that had been vomited into the Coogee pool on Anzac Day by a Tiger shark – the Superintendent assumed that a range of talents would be needed if the investigation was to have any chance of success. The two men he assigned to take charge complemented each other in important ways.

Both officers were detective-sergeants in their late forties with over ten years experience in the CIB. Frank Matthews, born in Bangor, Ireland, in 1888, was tall, had piercing eyes, and was beginning to put on weight in his middle age. He'd joined the New South Wales police as a uniformed officer just before the first world war. Leonard Frank Allmond was a year older than Matthews, and had been born in Seven-hampton, England. Before enlisting in the New South Wales police in 1915 he had served for four-and-a-half years as a uniformed police constable in Wales, and there was a touch of the friendly English 'bobby' about him.

Matthews was no visionary, but he had a messianic zeal for his police work. He could be expected to drive himself and his colleagues ruthlessly as he pursued any traces of the missing man.

Allmond, too, was extremely hard working. But he was more thoughtful than his colleague, more imaginative as well, which might enable him to detect evidence that the straight-forward Matthews would overlook. It was a feature of his police work that might be particularly significant in an inves-tigation that no one really knew how to begin.

Prior had another strong reason for linking the two offi-cers. If the remainder of Smith's body was never found, the success of the investigation would depend upon the ability of the police to obtain statements from potential witnesses. He considered Matthews and Allmond an ideal combination for this purpose.

The Superintendent likened police interrogations to performances by an orchestra. They often required fine tuning, with police officers being called upon to work in harmony, playing differently prescribed roles to achieve the best results. Allmond's gentler manner would serve well in dealings with individuals who'd had little previous contact with police. Matthew's tougher, confrontational stance, on the other hand, could menace even experienced criminals into admissions they would later regret.

Above all, Prior saw the two detective-sergeants as

seasoned exponents of a style of interrogation he regarded as a pinnacle of forensic art, used in situations where case hardened individuals were to be subjected to intense police questioning. Matthews would make threats and act aggressively, with the aim of upsetting the suspect's equilibrium. If this failed to bring satisfactory results, 'friendly cop' Allmond would step from the wings. The suspect might then 'confide' in the second officer to avoid being bullied once more by his more aggressive colleague.

The Superintendent didn't envisage that this tactic would be called on in the early stages of the investigation. In time, however, he reckoned, the interrogation of some of Jim Smith's less salubrious friends and associates could become the key to unravelling the mystery of his disappearance.

Meanwhile, Prior left Matthews and Allmond in no doubt that they faced an extremely tall order in pursuing their investigation: the dearth of evidence was probably without parallel in the long history of Sydney CIB investigations. As a student of crime, he reminded them that they could take comfort and inspiration from a few police success stories overseas. In one famous case in the United States, a Harvard professor had been convicted of murder although only the victim's false teeth remained after his body had been destroyed in a laboratory furnace. In England, a medical practitioner had been sent to the gallows even though only a few pieces of his deceased wife's flesh had ever been discovered. But for every successful investigation like this, Prior knew, there were many others where law enforcement agencies had been unable to overcome the obstacles presented by a shortage of physical evidence.

Chapter 11

THE GLADESVILLE CLUE

If Prior's special investigators were ever optimistic of a quick breakthrough in the shark arm mystery, their hopes were soon dashed. They were soon out on the beat, tramping the streets of an outlying Sydney suburb. It was detective work in one of its most common forms – time-consuming, soullessly repetitious, without the saving grace that it would necessarily serve a useful purpose. Each day, for long hours, the officers knocked on doors at homes and business premises, trying to find someone who could confirm Jim Smith's presence in early April.

For the time being, they had no alternative. Almost overnight the news of the discovery of the arm had denuded Sydney of key witnesses who might have assisted the investigation. Reginald Holmes had left town even before the arm's identity had been publicly confirmed. The boatbuilder had departed for Melbourne on a boat that took several days to reach the Victorian capital, without giving any plausible explanation for his departure to family or friends. Mystery also surrounded the whereabouts of one of Smith's closest friends and confidantes, a man called Patrick Brady. His family said they did not know where he had gone.

One slender clue came from a visit Matthews and Allmond paid to Smith's family home at Gladesville, where they interviewed Gladys Smith and her mother, Johanna Molloy. The two women did all they could to assist the officers, but it soon became clear that the missing man had often kept his immediate family in the dark about many of his activities.

Gladys Smith was obviously distressed, but she also seemed resigned about her husband's fate. She had coped for years with his unsettled lifestyle, hardly approving but unable to change him. In other households, a husband's frequent absences would have given concern, but Gladys had learned to endure the times he had gone off for days on end without explanation. She was quick to stress that she had not suspected him of being unfaithful to her on these occasions. Matthews and Allmond didn't see cause to doubt her.

The relationship between Jim and Gladys was typical of many Australians at the time. Jim spent his social life with men: in hotel bars, billiard saloons and, when he had money, at the races. Gladys was a devoted homemaker who mainly mixed with her female neighbours and friends. When she had a little spare money she went to the 'pictures' with her mother or son, or occasionally as a special treat with one or two of her 'girl friends'. For the rest, she told the police, she and her husband got on well enough, except when he returned home after drinking with his mates. Then 'he would be all right if he was left alone'.

Gladys could offer only second-hand knowledge of where Jim might have gone after he was seen at home for the last time. She was away when he left. On the night of Sunday 7 April he walked her down to catch a tram to Balmain, which was conveniently connected to their suburb by the Gladesville Bridge across the Parramatta River. She had been off to spend the night with a woman friend. Gladys recalled waving to Jim as the tram gathered speed, and noticing that he waved back. She'd confidently expected him to be at Batemans Road when she returned the next morning, as Jim had told her that an arrangement made for him to take charge of a fishing expedition over the next few days had fallen through. But when she got back, he was gone.

At first, she said, she wasn't greatly concerned by his absence. Her worries were further allayed by one of her neighbours, a Mrs Cruwys, who lived in an adjoining street. Mrs Cruwys occasionally took messages for her friends without telephones, and received a call about Jim a few days after he was last seen at home. Mrs Cruwys told Gladys that the message was delivered in a gruff male voice she didn't recognise. The man said: 'Tell Mrs Smith that Mr Smith will not be home until Monday night.' The caller then hung up without identifying himself or saying from where he was calling. Mrs Cruwys, however, guessed that the call was made in the Sydney metropolitan area, as there was no indication of a trunk line connection.

Gladys became more worried when Monday passed and her husband did not reappear. She made inquiries about his possible whereabouts. One person she contacted was Gregory Vaughan, the real estate agent who had been the dummy owner of the *Pathfinder*, whom she thought might have given Jim some seafaring work. But Vaughan scoffed at the suggestion, although he admitted seeing Jim at least once during the week before he disappeared. For two weeks more Gladys rebuffed her brother-in-law's urgings to report her husband missing. Her reason for this, she explained, was the fear that this might cause him trouble with the police.

Johanna Molloy, Gladys's mother, was a widow who had lived with the Smiths for eighteen months. She declined to tell the detectives her age, but otherwise seemed to be as forthcoming as she could in her dealings with them. Allmond, in particular, warmed to her. She had obviously faced many hardships, but had a 'way with her' that the detective found appealing. She revealed an affection for the missing man, clearly relishing the way he had called her 'Mum' or 'Ma'.

Despite her move to Gladesville, Johanna Molloy had not given up the habits of a lifetime spent in the tenements of Sydney's inner suburbs. One of these, as she admitted without apology, was keeping a keen eye on activities in her immediate neighbourhood. She liked to peer into the street from behind semi-closed curtains at the front of the house. Her curiosity enabled her to confirm that Jim Smith did not arrange to leave home until the morning of 8 April.

At about nine that morning, she remembered, she heard voices outside and looked from the curtains to see her son-in-law talking to someone across the picket fence that divided the Smith residence from Batemans Road. Jim Smith, she recalled, was leaning over in a way that suggested he was talking to a child. Disappointingly for the two sergeants, she hadn't been able to discover who this was. She moved back from the curtains when she guessed that her son-in-law was preparing to return inside, not wanting him to think she was spying on him.

When he returned inside, Johanna Molloy reported, Jim Smith had a broad grin on his face and a few silver coins in one hand. He made no mention of the identity of his visitor.

He told his mother-in-law that he was going fishing with a 'person of means' from another state and that the coins were to pay his fare to join him. He said that his immediate destination was south of Sydney, and that the boat they would be using was moored on Port Hacking, an inland waterway adjoining Cronulla.

Smith was ready to leave within half an hour, dressed in a light grey suit, clean blue shirt with a collar, and tan shoes he carefully polished. He also put on a grey felt hat that he took off a peg near the front door. He grabbed from a cupboard a small, brown, broken-clasped leather kitbag that contained shaving gear and other belongings, telling Johanna that he would be away for a few days. She recalled that he said, 'Goodbye Ma,' when he opened the front door. With another grin on his face he told her that the 'weather's fine and we should have a good time'. His mother-in-law called out to him jokingly to be 'careful of sharks'. 'I'll be okay,' he replied and added, 'Don't you worry either,' as he hurried to the front gate to catch a tram, grasping the handle of his kitbag in one hand.

The detectives were disappointed that Smith's mother-in-law was unable to give them more precise details of his planned destination on the morning of 8 April. It was hardly a great breakthrough to learn that he had probably gone to Cronulla. At the time, the town and its surroundings were still semi-rural in character, with a large floating population of visitors who used the many holiday cottages and shacks that were scattered in isolated bushland settings well away from the main town centre. Some visitors preferred to rent the fully-equipped pleasure boats moored in the neighbourhood. It could take weeks of patient investigation to determine whether Jim Smith had been setting out for one of these shacks or boats.

In the absence of other clues, however, the officers decided that their only choice was to organise a full-scale search at Cronulla in the hope of finding traces of the missing man's presence in the neighbourhood a month earlier. As soon as they returned to Central Street from Gladesville, Matthews and Allmond began enlisting new members for their team.

The next day they set out for Cronulla. Each officer, understandably, carried a picture of Jim Smith. But Matthews and Allmond made sure that officers also carried photographs of the boxer's crony, Patrick Brady.

Chapter 12

TELEPHONE PADDY

The idiosyncrasies of some malefactors betray their involvement in a crime as indelibly as do their fingerprints. Patrick
Brady was well known to the police at Central Street for
several eccentricities. One was his delight in reciting quotations from literature, including the works of Shakespeare,
even when under interrogation. Another was his habit of tele-
phoning or writing to his victims, or others who might be
harmed by his criminal activities, assuring them that all was
well. No one knew whether he did this out of bravado or to
purge his conscience. But it was such a common trait of his
that he came to be known to the Sydney CIB as 'Telephone
Paddy'.

When delivering his messages on the telephone, Brady
always spoke in a gruff voice, just like the person who had
rung Mrs Cruwys. As with her mysterious caller, he never
identified himself, not even by a false name. The detective-
sergeants' suspicion that he had made the call was bolstered
when Gladys Smith told them that Brady was one of a
handful of Smith's acquaintances who had been given Mrs
Cruwys's telephone number.

The police already knew that Jim Smith and Patrick Brady had been friends for a long time. Until they learned of the call to Mrs Cruwys, they believed the relationship between the two men to have been mainly social. Brady and Smith were of much the same age, and seemed to enjoy drinking in hotel bars and playing billiards together. The call to Mrs Cruwys, however, inferred that Brady had in some way been involved in his old friend's disappearance. It left the police confused: there was nothing in Brady's record to suggest that he was likely to have engaged in violence against Jim Smith, even if their friendship had waned.

If Patrick Brady had any great claim to fame with the police, it centred on his activities as a forger. His ability to copy signatures became so well known that his services were often sought beyond the boundaries of New South Wales. It was a skill he had perfected as a member of the Australian army in Europe during the first world war when, to the acclaim of his mates, he had produced false signatures on leave passes. Members of his unit boasted that his forgeries were never detected. Some years later, after his return to Australia, Brady took to forging as his occupation, mostly avoiding prosecution except on two occasions when he had been sent to gaol.

Despite his involvement in crime, police had never known Brady to have much propensity for violence. His forging was a sedentary job in which he worked alone, spending weeks perfecting copies of signatures that fooled even their original makers. He had only been known to act violently in occasional drunken brawls, when little harm had come to the participants.

Over the years Brady had become a guru of sorts among

the criminal fraternity in Newtown, Balmain and, most particularly, Rozelle. This was his own personal fiefdom: he was born and bred there, his parents lived there, and his three sisters and two brothers were raised in the area. He had strong local connections with church dignitaries and politicians, which sometimes enabled him to help his friends in times of difficulty.

The rest of Brady's family were hard-working and honest. His parents had emigrated from Ireland. His father had been secretary of a Hibernian lodge for many years, and a respected figure in the local Roman Catholic Church. Brady, by contrast, had been sent to a state reformatory for five years in 1905 at the age of twelve, after being convicted for stealing. It was the beginning of a strangely ambivalent lifestyle, in which he steered an erratic path towards and away from a life of crime, aided in the latter course by his family and later by his wife, Grace.

Brady learned to live by his wits at an early age after escaping from reform school, where he had developed a love of reading. He disappeared into the outback of New South Wales, where he worked in shearing sheds and took other odd jobs until he was seventeen, when he could no longer be held in custody as a juvenile offender. This experience toughened him physically and mentally. He continued to work as a shearer and in other rural occupations, with occasional visits to his family in Sydney, until he enlisted in the Australian army.

On his return to Australia after four-and-a-half years of military service, Brady, like Jim Smith, found work scarce for a person with his limited education. He had some accumulated pay and a small pension – after being permanently injured by a kick from a horse during his military service –

and took up one of the few opportunities for advancement open to him. He became an illegal bookmaker. One disastrous day he failed to balance his wagering transactions satisfactorily. By nightfall he was left owing large sums to several clients without any means of paying them. In the local vernacular, he had the prospect of 'Sydney or the bush'.

Most in Brady's situation would simply have opted for the bush, leaving the city with debts unpaid. The legends which surrounded Brady, and which helped to make him an increasingly popular figure among local criminals, began with his reaction to this situation. Brady was no 'welsher', as he immediately demonstrated. He sold his new home and disposed of all of his family's furniture. When this wasn't enough to meet his debts, he devoted a portion of all other income he earned to making up the shortfall, until every winning bet was paid out in full.

Soon after, his local reputation was further enhanced. In 1922 he became an itinerant meat vendor. He joined the ranks of other hawkers, such as the 'Rabbit-ohs' with their strings of rabbits, selling his wares from a horse-drawn cart around the streets of Rozelle. It was an uncertain occupation at best. On hot days, meat could quickly become fly-blown, or go bad under the hessian covering the back of his cart.

The collapse of Brady's new enterprise, however, had nothing to do with the quality of his meat. He was charged by the police for being a receiver of stolen goods in the form of a set of scales he was using in his business. It was common local knowledge that Brady hadn't known that the scales had been stolen. However, he refused adamantly to 'drop the bucket' on the acquaintance from whom he'd bought them, proclaiming to his friends that he was no 'copper's nark'. As a result he was convicted of the offence, and went to gaol for twelve weeks until the combined influences of a local priest, a member of parliament and the Mayor of Balmain secured his early release.

This was the first time Brady spent in an adult prison. The experience hardened his outlook on life, and brought him into everyday contact with 'graduates' from the state's prison system. Such acquaintances helped to consolidate his relationships with other malefactors who lived around Rozelle.

If Brady became a hard man, there was one area in which police knew him to be sensitive. He was protective toward his family. His parents, brothers and sisters never deserted him over the years. They raised bail for him, visited him in prison, found money for him when he failed as an illegal bookmaker, and defended him when he was charged with receiving stolen goods. In return, he sought to ensure at all costs that they were never tainted by their association with him. His greatest resentments and most vulnerable moments arose whenever it was suggested that his wife, Grace, had anything to do with his illegal activities.

Grace Brady was from a thrifty, hard-working Catholic family. Her first meeting with 'Pat', as she called her husband, had been outside their local parish church one Sunday after mass. They were married in the same church not long afterwards. Grace found solace in her religion, attending mass every Sunday, sometimes with her husband, invariably with their son John, who was eleven in 1935.

After their marriage, Grace never wavered in the support she gave her husband. She regarded his conviction in 1922 as the most 'calamitous' event in her life. She endured his time in prison, and was mostly forgiving towards him, despite her disapproval of much of what he did. Brady, in return, was intensely loyal to his wife. Only once throughout their married life had Grace suspected that her husband might be conducting an affair. Acting on a hunch, she had followed him to a remote location, and had discovered that he'd been merely playing cards and drinking beer with a group of cronies. She never mistrusted him again.

Police who dealt with Brady normally respected his desire to keep his family at arm's length from his criminal activities. But not every member of the CIB thought along these lines, as Allmond discovered in a discussion with Matthews after their visit to Gladesville. Matthews suggested that perhaps they should embroil Grace Brady in their inquiries, in the hope that her husband would then become more compliant in providing them with information. His partner's scheme troubled Allmond. He felt that the scheme could only be justified if Brady's wife or other members of his family became suspects in the mystery of Smith's disappearance. Otherwise, Allmond believed, the police could be accused of moral blackmail, and would be subjecting Grace and others to harassment and intimidation they did not deserve.

It was a subject on which the officers agreed to differ, at least for the time being, settling on a compromise. The police Shadow Squad would place Brady's wife and other members of his family under surveillance to see if they were attempting to contact him. Meanwhile, an all-out effort would be made to find any signs of the presence of Jim Smith or Patrick Brady in the vicinity of Cronulla in early April.

Chapter 13

A HOTEL CALLED CECIL

A commodious hotel called the Cecil, just away from the town centre, was one of the social centres of semi-rural Cronulla in 1935. It was much like a busy crossroads, overlooking the Pacific Ocean, but still just a short distance away from Gunnamatta Bay on the inland waterway of Port Hacking. One of its most popular amenities was a barn-like public bar where, according to the social conventions of the time, only males were allowed. Regular clientele included fishermen and other locals as well as holiday-makers.

Between five and six from Monday to Friday the bar became a seething mass of drinkers as compulsory closing time approached. They battled with each other to reach the island counter before the call of 'last drinks'. The melee was repeated on Saturday afternoons before the bar was securely shut down at six until the following Monday morning.

At other times, however, few customers were around and the bar took on a different character. It became a friendly place, despite the sickly green and cream tiles that lined the walls. Small tables and chairs were available for those who wanted to play dominoes and other games; others could drink quietly, seated on high-legged stools ranged around the island counter. During these calm periods the bar was presided over by a man called Harry Levi, an experienced barman who looked back nostalgically to the more civilised days before the first world war when bars were permitted to stay open much longer. He treated his customers as friends, trading gossip with regulars and helping visitors as best he could, directing them to the nearby depots where steam trams and buses provided transport to the city. Harry was a mine of local information, a conveyor of messages for his clientele, a confidante.

It took Matthews and Allmond almost a week to meet the barman after they began their inquiries at Cronulla. They originally made a call there when Harry wasn't in. After that, Matthews declared that the officers in the task force should not be seen in hotel bars when they were on duty. This command left officers tramping around the town with nothing to show for their efforts. At CIB headquarters Prior was almost ready to call off the Cronulla search as a futile exercise.

All this changed suddenly when a letter arrived in the post at the Smith home in Gladesville. It was addressed to the Smiths' son Raymond, and read: 'Son, keep your mother quiet. I am in a jam. I plead its OK. Call the cops off. Tell your Mum. I will have plenty soon. They want me for something in town. Never mind be a man.' The letter was signed, 'Your loving father Jim Smith,' and ended with a terse postscript: 'Destroy this.'

Gladys Smith and her mother read and re-read the letter, studied the signature and declared that it was genuine. For a few hours they believed that by some miracle Jim Smith was still alive, that he had survived the crude amputation of his left arm. At Central Street, however, the letter was viewed in a different light. Handwriting experts confirmed that the signature was a forgery, albeit a good one. In hurried consultation with Prior, Matthews and Allmond agreed that the letter was further evidence that their long-time adversary, Telephone Paddy, was on the job.

Police suspected that the letter was intended to lure them away from Cronulla, but it had the opposite effect. 'I'll call bloody Paddy's bluff,' Prior told the two detective-sergeants. He ordered his subordinates to step up their inquiries at Cronulla, offering them more assistance if they needed it. He upbraided Matthews for putting the hotels in the district off-limits to his officers, reminding the detective-sergeant that they were natural meeting places for men like Brady and Smith. 'They spend more time there than they do at home,' he told them.

Some believed it was the Superintendent's sixth sense that directed Matthews and Allmond back to the Cecil hotel and Harry Levi. But those most in the know realised that Prior's understanding of the social habits of men like Brady and Smith was the key. Nor did they overlook the fact that Matthews and Allmond themselves enjoyed a drink in a hotel bar, provided Matthews believed he had the Superintendent's approval.

Without hesitation, Levi pointed to a police photograph of Brady and nominated him as a man he knew as 'Williams' who had visited the Cecil's public bar several times in early April. He also recognised Jim Smith. Their presence in the bar was fixed in his memory because of an acrimonious dispute. In the mid-afternoon of 8 April, the day Smith was last seen at home, the barman was abused by a customer who claimed that Levi had cheated his employer by putting the money paid for a drink into his own pocket and not the bar till. Levi recounted how he had been grateful when Jim Smith came to his aid, declaring that the obstreperous customer was mistaken. 'He may have saved my job,' Levi told the detectives.

Levi remembered Brady being in the bar on several occasions during the week before 8 April. After passing conversations with him, he'd gained the impression that Brady was staying somewhere in the neighbourhood. On the Saturday before Monday, 8 April, Smith arrived at the bar in the early afternoon, looking for the man Levi knew as 'Williams'. When he didn't appear Smith left, saying that he was returning to the city, and asking Levi to give 'Williams' a message to telephone Smith at a bar in a hotel at Enmore. Levi handed the message to 'Williams' later that day.

On the afternoon of 8 April, Brady was the first of the two men to appear in the bar. He'd left a message with Levi for Smith, asking the former boxer to meet him at a nearby wharf. The barman assumed this meant that Brady had a boat waiting there. Not long after, Brady returned and was soon joined by Smith.

Levi had no idea where Brady had been living. It could have been in rented premises anywhere within a radius of several kilometres, perhaps even further out if he had a boat at his disposal. Alternatively, he might have been staying in one of the many boats with living quarters that were available for leasing in the vicinity. The detectives were puzzled that on the two occasions Smith had arrived at the Cecil he hadn't known where Brady was staying. The barman could not remember the precise time that Brady and Smith had left the Cecil. He thought he'd seen them at 'about five o'clock or a quarter past five'. But he'd been overtaken by the frantic rush for last drinks before closing time, and couldn't be sure whether they had been there longer. On this count, Levi referred the detectives to two of his regular customers, Albert Ward and Gordon Dall, whom he'd noticed spending time with Brady and Smith during the afternoon.

Ward, who explained that he was an insurance agent who did most of his business in Balmain and nearby, was able to confirm that Smith had been at the Cecil on the afternoon of 8 April. Ward said he'd met Smith casually in hotel bars many times over the last fifteen years. During the afternoon of 8 April, together with Dall, he played dominoes with Brady and Smith. He remembered: 'We played a four handed game. We played two games.' He told the disappointed detective that the conversation between the four men had dealt with 'nothing in particular'. But it did seem, after detailed police questioning, that Brady and Smith had deliberately avoided any mention of what they were doing at Cronulla.

Dall, on the other hand, had exchanged a brief, private conversation with Smith that the police found more revealing. Dall suggested to the visitor that, if he was still at Cronulla on the following Saturday, they might have another game. Smith had replied that he was going home that night. Matthews and Allmond reckoned this might have been no more than a cover-up to hide what he was doing in the neighbourhood.

Like Harry Levi, neither man was able to say when Brady and Smith had finally left the Cecil. Both hated the last frantic rush for drinks, and had left the bar soon after it began. To the best of their recollection, however, they thought that the two men had still been there at five or a little after.

Matthews and Allmond long remembered their visit to the bar at the Cecil as their first real breakthrough in the case of the Tiger shark and the tattooed limb. The missing man had clearly been with Patrick Brady on the last day anyone so far had been able to state that he was alive. On their way back to Sydney that night, however, they still faced the gruelling prospect of days or weeks tramping around Cronulla after further traces of Brady and Smith. But, as Allmond said wryly to his dour colleague, at least they had an excuse for spending more time in the public bar of the Cecil.

Chapter 14

WATERFRONT COTTAGE

An understanding of human nature is a boon to criminal investigation, as William Prior had proved once again by directing Matthews and Allmond to revisit the Cecil hotel. The next day, Frank Matthews demonstrated that military-like planning can be of equal value.

Overnight he prepared listings of as many letting agencies in the Cronulla region as he could find. They were all to be visited, together with any others the police discovered. Every employee of every agency was to be shown the photographs of Patrick Brady and Jim Smith.

The operation quickly surpassed even Matthews's expectations. Within a short time he was seated with Allmond in the waiting room of a Cronulla real estate agent named Percival Alley, who had recognised a photograph of Patrick Brady as a man he knew as 'Williams'. Alley was preparing to rummage through a large diary on his desk as the officers were ushered into his office. The diary contained a brief timetable of events relating to Brady. As Alley elaborated, the detectives leaned forward in growing excitement.

The real estate agent had first met Brady in the third week in March. He told the detectives that the forger had wanted a cottage by the water, one with a boat so he could do some fishing. He had sent Brady off to inspect a cottage called Cored Joy on Taloombi Street, about two kilometres south of the main town with direct access to Gunnamatta Bay. Brady had agreed to take it after finding the rent included the use of a small rowboat housed in a shed at the rear of the cottage. Alley recalled: 'He said he wanted it for two or three or possibly eight weeks.'

The detectives were unable to conceal their disappointment when Alley told them he had only received two weeks' rent and assumed that Brady had left the premises by 8 April. For a few moments, it appeared that the telephone teaser had given up his tenancy before meeting Jim Smith at the Cecil on the last afternoon the police knew the missing man had been seen alive. But the officers' dismay was transformed when the real estate agent went on to describe a visit by Brady to the agency on 9 April. Late in the morning, Brady had appeared at Alley's office unshaven and looking as if he had not slept the night before. Saying hardly a word, he had handed over sufficient rent money to stay at the waterfront cottage for the rest of the week. He had re-appeared at the office on the following Saturday. As the real estate agent recounted: 'He told me that he would not require the cottage for any further term.'

Alley told the police that he suspected Brady had not stayed at Cored Joy for the whole of the week after 9 April. Three days after the rental period had finally expired, the keys to the cottage had been returned to Alley by a bus driver who had been to the city. They'd been handed to the driver there by someone Alley presumed was Brady.

The detectives grabbed the keys from Alley, and set

out for Cored Joy. The cottage stood in an isolated bushland setting, surrounded by eucalyptus trees and native scrub. It was little more than a two-bedroomed holiday shack at the foot of a steep incline. It was reached from the street only by a narrow set of wooden steps. Inside, everything appeared to be in an immaculate condition, leaving the detectives with the sinking feeling that any traces of Brady's sojourn had disappeared. It was the same in the small shed at the rear. The partly-concreted floor had recently been washed down. The small rowboat looked as if it had been scrubbed down, too.

Back at the town centre, the detectives were even more disappointed to find that Alley had no idea of what had actually happened at the cottage during Brady's tenancy. He explained that he'd never been to Cored Joy while the forger was a tenant, and that he and Brady had always met at his office. In passing, however, the real estate agent mentioned that there was someone who might know more about Brady's time at the cottage. Its owner, he told the officers, was another real estate agent, Percival Forbes, whose office was in the suburb of Canterbury. The detectives noted down the address as Alley went on to say that Forbes frequently visited Cored Joy at the end of a tenancy to check that the cottage had been kept in good order.

The detectives' first impressions of Forbes gave them little hope he could help them much. He seemed obsessed by detail, describing how he'd purchased Cored Joy a few years previously, how he organised the letting of the cottage, and how members of his own family used it at times. But slowly, inch by nit-picking inch, Matthews and Allmond began to realise that the Canterbury real estate agent's concern with minutiae might fit another piece into the puzzle of the forger and the boxer.

Forbes was able to confirm beyond doubt that Brady had still been staying at Cored Joy on the day before Jim Smith was seen at home for the last time. From what he told the police, it also seemed clear that Brady had intended to be there on the following day and for the remainder of the week. Like Alley, Forbes originally believed that Brady had relinquished his tenancy after two weeks. He went to Cored Joy on Sunday 7 April to check on the state of the premises. To his surprise, he found Brady still ensconced there. Brady had introduced him to two women, explaining that they were his wife and sister. Forbes was told that two boys of about twelve playing near the water were Brady's son, John, and his nephew.

The finicky real estate agent had been pleased to see that the cottage was in excellent order. He noticed his rowboat floating on Gunnamatta Bay, tethered to the shore by a rope attached to an iron weight called a killick. He was told that the women and children planned to return to Sydney that night, but that Brady wanted to stay on for another week. The forger said he would spend most of his time fishing with friends who were coming from Sydney to join him. Forbes agreed to this arrangement and told Brady to pay the rent to Percival Alley later in the week.

The most startling of Forbes's revelations followed as he painstakingly went on to describe two visits he'd made to Cored Joy after Brady's departure. The first had been a few days later, the other soon after that.

On the first occasion, he was in a hurry to meet other commitments. He was especially gratified to see that the floors of the kitchen and living room had been scrupulously cleaned. Suddenly, almost spookily, he felt that something was wrong. He glanced around and realised that a metal trunk in the living room was not his. It was smaller than the one he used to store family possessions when tenants were using the cottage. He opened up the new one to find that the belongings were all still there, packed just as neatly as his family had left them in his own metal container.

He went out to the shed and found that his small rowboat had been used for fishing. There was a sickening smell coming from it, the source a long-dead fish that had been left in it. Part of one of the vessel's metal rowlocks was broken off, and there was no sign of the missing piece. The killick he had seen a few days before was also gone, replaced by a new one, which had never been used but was attached to the same old rope that had been tied to his. Some lead weights had disappeared from the shed.

On his second, longer visit to the waterfront cottage, Forbes discovered even more to confuse him. The walls of one of the bedrooms had obviously been carefully washed down without his knowledge. A kapok mattress had been replaced with another, and had been covered with an ordinary blanket instead of the Scotch rug that had been there previously. The rug had vanished, and so had two small mats that had been on the floor.

Before leaving, the real estate agent had collected what he believed was an empty kerosene tin. He told the police that he collected such items as scrap metal, which he sold from time to time. On his arrival home, he had found that the tin was not entirely empty. He then astounded Matthews and Allmond by saying that, when he poured out the contents, some of the liquid had been kerosene but the remainder had been a 'red substance'. Forbes told them he thought this substance was blood. He had experimented with the liquid to see if it would mingle with the kerosene. The red substance remained separate from the kerosene, clustering together in small beads of its own. The detectives were almost out of their chairs in excitement, but the pernickety real estate agent soon let them down. It was no longer possible to test whether the red substance was indeed blood. Forbes had poured the remainder of the liquid under one of the fruit trees in his backyard, burned out the kerosene tin, flattened it, placed it on his pile of scrap metal, and sold it.

It was time, the frustrated detectives realised, for a long, deep consultation with Superintendent Prior.

Chapter 15

JIGSAW PUZZLE

Matthews and Allmond told the Superintendent they had gathered bits of evidence that began to provide a possible outline of the demise of Jim Smith. But they lacked vital pieces. Certainly they didn't have enough of the picture to show it to any court.

All three men agreed that the discovery of Cored Joy turned the spotlight on Patrick Brady, rather than Reginald Holmes, as the person most likely to have been directly responsible for Jim Smith's disappearance. Percival Forbes's testimony helped flesh out a scenario in which the missing man died violently and his body was carefully disposed of.

The officers agreed that it was reasonable to speculate that Jim Smith had been killed in a bedroom at Cored Joy. This explained why the walls had been scrubbed down, and the kapok mattress, Scotch rug and two mats had been removed. Despite a minute examination of the bedroom, the police had not discovered any physical traces of blood. The red 'beads' in the kerosene tin Forbes had taken home had, of course, long since disappeared.

The officers also believed that it was reasonably safe to assume that Jim Smith's body had been dismembered at Cored

Joy. It seemed probable that his remains, minus the tattooed arm, had been stuffed in Forbes's metal trunk and carried away to be dumped, possibly in Gunnamatta Bay, with the missing heavy iron killick and the other weights as ballast. The rowlock on Forbes's rowboat had probably been broken while the trunk was being dumped in the water. The mattress, Scotch rug and missing mats had been destroyed, or buried at some remote spot, because they were covered with blood.

But this scenario still left the detectives confused about why the tattooed limb had been separated from the remainder of Jim Smith's body. One suggestion was that there had not been enough room in the metal trunk for all of the corpse. This was discounted by Matthews and Allmond, who had noted the Canterbury real estate agent's meticulous description of the dimensions of the lost trunk. Another view was that the arm could have been accidentally left out of the trunk in the haste to dispose of the missing man's body, then later tossed separately into the sea. Detective-Sergeant Allmond suggested another, more intriguing possibility.

Allmond told the meeting that, aside from his finger-prints, Jim Smith's tattoo was his most notable physical characteristic. His arm, therefore, might have been deliber-ately severed from his body for some ulterior purpose. Perhaps both arms had been amputated to prevent fingerprint identification. Alternatively, Smith's tattooed arm might have been cut off as proof that the seafaring boxer was well and truly dead. Prior in particular was prepared to take this grue-some possibility seriously. He reminded his colleagues that there were men in Sydney who would kill on demand for five hundred pounds or less, and that Smith's arm might have been the keepsake that would guarantee payment.

The three detectives were forced to admit that speculation like this remained the only justification for continuing their investigations. Criminal charges could be sustained if they found enough circumstantial evidence to enable inferences to be drawn on what had happened to Smith. But the onus on the police in these circumstances was extremely heavy, and Prior and his colleagues knew they needed far more evidence before they could even contemplate charging anyone over Smith's disappearance. The detectives were left with hard decisions as they planned their next moves.

Unless police could find the remainder of Jim Smith's body, it seemed unlikely that they would ever be able to demonstrate the exact cause of his death. Boldly, Superintendent Prior decided to take the unprecedented step of asking the Royal Australian Air Force to work with state maritime authorities in a bid to find Percival Forbes's missing trunk. Air force planes with police observers would scan Gunnamatta Bay for signs of the trunk, while boats with divers on board would be stationed below, ready to search the bed of the waterway at a signal from above. Meanwhile, pending the federal government's approval of this scheme, a group of divers would begin a systematic search of the waterway.

The three detectives were also worried about the lack of firm evidence linking Patrick Brady with the events they believed had taken place at Cored Joy. They could easily prove that the forger was in Cronulla at the time Jim Smith was last seen in the area. But this did not show that he was at the waterfront cottage when Jim Smith was killed there, if that had indeed been the boxer's fate. Similarly, there was nothing to indicate that Brady was associated with the disposal of Smith's body, nor any strong evidence that he'd been involved in replacing the metal trunk, the kapok mattress and the Scotch rug.

Pending the outcome of the official request for a full-scale search of the bed of Gunnamatta Bay, the three officers agreed that Cronulla should remain the focus of police inquiries. Once more, CIB officers would traipse the streets armed with photographs of Patrick Brady and Jim Smith. This time, however, they would extend their inquiries beyond the town centre, concentrating on the neighbourhood of Cored Joy.

The surveillance of Brady's family would also be intensified. For the time being, however, the detectives decided they did not want to apprehend him. They were confident that Brady was hiding out in Sydney, as the letter sent to Jim Smith's family had been posted from the metropolitan area. The Shadow Squad reported that Grace Brady and other members of Brady's family had been trailed to North Sydney, where the detectives believed he was living. But it was far better, the officers determined, to keep Brady 'on ice'. Prior wanted to let 'Paddy stew a little more', until the CIB had more concrete evidence at its disposal.

Chapter 16

AN EARLY MORNING JOURNEY

Just before seven on the morning after Jim Smith was seen at the Cecil hotel for the last time, a short, sturdy man approached a businessman near the main town centre of Cronulla. The businessman was Charles Cooper, the proprietor of a petrol station, who also ran a one-car taxi service from the same location. When later looking at a police photograph, he recognised the man who had approached him as Patrick Brady. Cooper recalled that Brady 'had a couple of days growth of beard, I would say'. He went on: 'He looked as if he had been out all night, or on the booze, he did not look as if he had come out of a bed.'

Brady said that he urgently required a taxi to take him to the city. The garage proprietor explained that Bill Brown, the driver of his cab, was not due to arrive until some time later. But Cooper suggested that, if Brady needed him quickly, he should go to Brown's house to fetch him. A few minutes later the taxi-driver found Brady at his front door looking as if he 'had been out to a drinking party and that he had no sleep and was tired'. His visitor said that he must get to Sydney immediately: his wife had suddenly become critically ill there.

The detectives' meetings with Cooper and Brown helped

justify their decision to keep Cronulla central to their inquiries. But their success did not come immediately. There were a few desperate hours when it seemed that the speculation they had engaged in with the Superintendent was altogether misplaced. The detective-sergeants visited Cored Joy, and discovered a palpable error in their calculations. On checking the dimensions of Forbes's rowing boat, they found that it was too small to have transported both a grown man and the missing trunk. Prior was contacted to halt his plans for the full-scale search of Gunnamatta Bay. The detectives' equilibrium was restored, however, by a report from an officer who had been visiting houses around Cored Joy.

At a house called Maisieville, on Taloombi Street, two people made disclosures about Patrick Brady's stay in the neighbourhood. One was a fisherman coincidentally named James Smith. The other was his wife. They confirmed that Brady was in the area well after the time the other Jim Smith was last seen. Brady borrowed a motorised skiff from them for a period beginning before 8 April and ending about a week later. The Smiths were not sure of the precise dates.

The plan for the search of the bed of Gunnamatta Bay was immediately reinstated. The skiff was big enough to have carried Forbes's trunk plus a couple of passengers on board. More troubling for the detectives, however, was the new possibility that the container could have been dumped well away from Cored Joy, perhaps in the deep, often turbulent water where Port Hacking joins with the Pacific Ocean. If it was there, it would probably never be found. The Smiths' powerful vessel might also have been used to convey items missing from Cored Joy to the untracked wilderness of the Royal National Park on the south shore of Port Hacking.

The information from the Smiths of Taloombi Street went further, rivetting the attention of Matthews and Allmond. The Smiths related that Brady called in after 9 April, reporting that the skiff's anchor and the manilla rope attached to it had been lost, without giving any explanation. He promised to replace the items and they found him as good as his word when the skiff was returned. The detectives grew excited: the lost manilla rope could have been the one tied to the severed limb. It was possible, too, that the arm was weighed down with the anchor. They could be moving in on proof of a connection between Brady and the arrival of the tattooed arm in the Coogee pool.

For the time being, however, the thrust of the police investigation changed dramatically as a result of testimony about Patrick Brady's early morning taxi ride. The journey began at about 7.30, by which time there was another passenger, a war veteran named Lloyd Cook, who was on his way to a government medical clinic. Cook told police he first noticed Brady waiting for driver Bill Brown near Cooper's garage, his left hand stuffed in the pocket of his overcoat. Cook put this down to cold weather until he found that his fellow passenger's hand stayed in his coat throughout the trip to Sydney. He was even more surprised when Brady leaned over awkwardly to use his right hand to pull down a window blind, and struggled to unbutton his coat with it. Cook noticed that one of Brady's shoelaces was undone. He was sure his fellow passenger knew this, as he glanced down at it several times. But he made no effort to do it up, presumably, Cook guessed, because this would have required two hands and Brady had no intention of exposing his left one.

Brady and Cook quickly established a rapport, reminiscing

about wartime experiences. But Cook recalled that his companion was reticent about his stay at Cronulla. All he said was that he had been fishing at Port Hacking until about four in the morning and had not had time to shave and change before finding a taxi to take him to his ailing wife in Sydney.

Bill Brown found his journey to Sydney with Brady an equally strange encounter. Through his rear-vision mirror he noticed Brady glancing back anxiously at the road many times, as if he believed someone might be following him. But most disconcerting was Brady's uncertainty about his destination, which seemed hardly compatible with his earlier plea that he urgently needed to reach his sick wife. After dropping off Cook, Brady directed the taxi-driver to head for a suburb south of central Sydney. But when they got there, his passenger suddenly, without explanation, ordered him to drive elsewhere. They drove around aimlessly for a time before Brady directed the taxi over the harbour bridge. At its northern outlet, his passenger then directed Brown through several streets he obviously knew quite well.

Matthews and Allmond sat bolt upright when the taxi-driver revealed where he finally delivered Brady. He had good reason to remember it. When he pulled up outside, he found that Brady had no money to pay his fare. He feared a ruse when his passenger rushed inside saying that he would return with the money, and took note of the house for possible future reference. It was, he recalled, a prestigious residence on Lower Bay View Street, McMahon's Point. From Brown's description, the two detectives recognised the home of Reginald Holmes. From what Bill Brown added it was clear that Brady was well-known inside. Brady returned to the cab after a few minutes with a clutch of money in one hand.

For Matthews, Allmond and William Prior, this evidence of a relationship between Brady and Holmes came as a complete surprise. Unshaven, bedraggled, bearing every sign that he had undergone a traumatic experience, Brady had sought out Reginald Holmes. Suddenly the North Sydney boatbuilder was back in the frame. And Patrick Brady seemed even more likely to be the key to unlocking the case of the tattooed limb.

Chapter 17

TAXI-CAB MERRY-GO-ROUND

In 1935 taxis were a regular form of transport for the majority of Sydney's inhabitants who, like Patrick Brady, had no private cars. Sydney's urban sprawl was already growing bigger than that of cities with larger populations, such as London and New York, and taxis were a simple way to get from one place in the city to another. But Brady also tried to use them as a way of hiding his tracks when he went from place to place, overlooking that he was actually blazing a conspicuous trail.

Including his journey from Cronulla on the morning of 8 April, Matthews and Allmond discovered that over three days Brady had made use of taxis in the Sydney metropolitan area on five occasions. All rides but one involved trips to or from Cronulla. The exception was a night call to McMahon's Point, when Brady was again dropped off at the home of Reginald Holmes.

The records of these taxi trips did not give a complete picture of Brady's movements over the period. The police had no detailed knowledge of everywhere that he might have gone. It was clear, however, that the forger was a much-travelled person during the two days after his meeting with Jim Smith at the Cecil hotel, and that he spent considerable time at Cored Joy or nearby during this period. Brady returned by cab to Cronulla after being dropped at McMahon's Point by Bill Brown. The next morning he was driven in another taxi to the same destination, presumably after going back to the city some time before by other transport, with an eighteen-hour gap between cab rides. Later the same day he travelled back to the city in another taxi.

Tracing Brady's peregrinations added more to the police knowledge of his activities than just a record of his movements around the Sydney metropolitan area. The testimony of his drivers fuelled speculation that he was not the only person involved in happenings at Cored Joy. The evidence of one driver went further, providing a substantial evidentiary link between Brady and events that appeared to relate directly to Jim Smith's disappearance.

During their early morning taxi ride, Bill Brown noticed that Brady glanced around on a number of occasions as if he was fearful of being followed. He awkwardly drew a side blind on the taxi – left hand still thrust in one of his coat pockets – even though the autumn sun was barely up. The evidence of the taxi-driver who drove Brady back to Cronulla later the same day inferred that he was anxious about whether there might be people waiting for him at Cored Joy. The cab-driver told the police that the forger alighted from the taxi some distance from the waterfront cottage and walked along the shoreline to reach it, struggling with parcels of food he had bought. It looked like he was preparing to reconnoitre around Cored Joy before venturing inside again.

The next morning, after returning to Sydney by means

the police had not ascertained, Brady was picked up in a cab driven by Bert McGowan, a forthright fellow with an eye for detail. Brady boarded the taxi at South Kensington, where his wife and son were staying with one of his sisters. He first told McGowan that he only needed him for a short trip, and instructed the driver to take him to a location where, he said, he would be met by a man in a private car.

When the vehicle did not appear Brady became irate, exasperated by the failure of the man to arrive. He directed McGowan on a meandering journey among second-hand shops. He bought a kapok mattress at one and a metal trunk at another, and took them in the cab to Cored Joy.

Before this news, the police had evidence enough that Brady had been around Cored Joy when Jim Smith had disappeared. The law, however, requires more than a person's mere presence in the vicinity of a crime to prove criminal liability. There must at the very least be evidence that the accused person had the opportunity to participate in a criminal act. McGowan's story did not help to prove in any way that Brady had harmed Jim Smith. But it did provide, as Matthews and Allmond jubilantly recognised, the foundations of a credible case that Brady had been involved in the disposal of Jim Smith's body.

McGowan's observations on his trip with Brady also bolstered the detectives' suspicion that the forger had not been solely responsible for Smith's disappearance. McGowan told the detectives that Brady was unable to handle the metal trunk successfully without the help of another person. Brady needed McGowan's help to carry the trunk from the second-hand shop and tie it on the rear of the cab. At Cored Joy Brady again needed the taxi-driver's help to manoeuvre it down the steps to the cottage. Despite the inconvenience, Brady refused McGowan's offer to help carry the trunk into the waterfront cottage. If Brady was incapable of moving the trunk when it was empty, he would plainly have needed at least one other person to transport it when most of Jim Smith's body was inside.

McGowan's testimony raised another puzzle for the detective-sergeants, one which they realised they had no chance of solving for the time being. When he picked up Brady, the taxi-driver noticed that Brady was carrying a medium-sized, brown leather kitbag. He kept it close by in the taxi and even took it with him when he went to the second-hand shops. The bag was still beside Brady when he paid the taxi-driver near the unopened front door of Cored Joy. Later that day Brady returned to Sydney in another cab: the driver was prepared to swear that the forger no longer had the bag with him.

Where had the bag gone? There had been no sign of it later at Cored Joy – Percival Forbes certainly would have noticed if it was there after Brady left the cottage. The police had no indication that he had ever carried it again. Matthews and Allmond couldn't help speculating that it was the same bag that Jim Smith carried when he left home for the last time. But it was a common kind of bag in Sydney at the time. If it had been at Cored Joy earlier, Brady did not carry it with him to and from Cronulla on 9 April when he started his day with his early morning taxi ride with Bill Brown. 'Maybe he had the arm in it,' Allmond joked to Matthews, and the detectives laughed at what seemed fanciful conceit. They agreed, however, that the bag would have been large enough to hold the arm.

Later that same day, Brady failed to meet a cab from Sydney he had ordered to meet him near a park not far from the centre of Cronulla. He telephoned ahead to have the cab stopped at a toll booth on the bridge at Tom Ugly's Point, on the way to Sydney, and said that he would grab a bus and catch up with the cab-driver there. On his arrival, however, he asked the cabbie to wait, and went into the bar of a nearby hotel. At first he looked around as if he was expecting to meet someone there, then he made enquiries to see if a person he was expecting in a private car was there to meet him. When he gathered that the man had not appeared, Brady left with the taxi-driver. Matthews and Allmond conjectured that the men who failed to materialise at the two meetings were probably one and the same.

The detectives also remarked that Brady seemed to become flush with money after his early morning trip to Reginald Holmes's North Sydney home. He paid hefty cab fares to Brown, McGowan and other drivers, and purchased the mattress, trunk and other items without difficulty, even though he clearly had little cash on the morning of 8 April. There seemed no doubt that the source of some of this was Holmes.

The nexus between the forger and the North Sydney boatbuilder was confirmed by other taxi-drivers. One reported driving Brady to Holmes's residence on the night of 12 April. He testified that Brady took great care to hide his presence in the cab, directing it away from main thoroughfares and demanding that the car's inside light be turned off, even though it was normal to leave the light on to show the vehicle was under hire. The detectives also discovered from another taxi-driver that the liaison between the two men stretched back to before Jim Smith's disappearance. The cabbie remembered taking Brady to the Holmeses' residence twice in the week before 8 April. Once he waited at night in Lower Bay View Street for an hour and a half before Brady returned to be driven to the city.

Intriguing possibilities had been opened up by their investigation, but it had also come to a dead end. It seemed that the police had exhausted every means of finding evidence at Cronulla, at least until the aerial search for Forbes's trunk. The information on the relationship between Brady and Holmes was potent, but shadowy. The detectives decided that the time had come when the only way to advance the investigation was to seek out Brady and bring him to Central Street for questioning. Reginald Holmes would soon need to be approached, too, if only to allay the growing suspicion that he'd also been involved in foul play at the waterfront cottage.

Both men, the officers realised, would be formidable adversaries: Brady because of his experienced, hard-bitten manner in his dealings with the police, Holmes because he would have an array of well-paid legal talent to support him. But without verbal admissions from either or both of them the police were a long way from producing a credible case about the events they were certain had taken place at Cored Joy in the second week of April.

Chapter 18

OFF THE ICE

On a dark evening in the middle of May a stealthy group of police officers, led by Matthews and Allmond, approached a ground-floor flat in North Sydney at an establishment called The Pines. The detective-sergeants stayed near the entrance while two detective-constables moved to the rear of the building. Matthews pounded on the front door. Grace Brady opened it gingerly. The two burly officers rushed past her, and Allmond shouted: 'We are detectives! The place is surrounded!'

They found Patrick Brady standing near a bedroom window that opened onto a small back yard. He looked the detectives up and down, and laconically asked, 'Yes, what's doing?'

Brady stood defiantly near the wall for a few moments. He was wearing an overcoat over a pyjama coat and ordinary trousers. It looked as though he'd heard a noise outside and had hurriedly dressed for escape, then seen the other police waiting at the rear of the flat. Resigned, he obeyed Matthews's order to dress, and was then bundled out of the flat by the two detective-constables without being allowed a moment of farewell with his wife.

It was an anti-climax to a day of frenetic activity for the

detectives as they had made detailed preparations to take Brady 'off the ice'. They knew his whereabouts from the members of the police Shadow Squad, who had followed Grace Brady to the premises. Before they finally decided that the day was right to apprehend the forger, they had ascertained that divers at Cronulla had found no trace of the metal trunk in Gunnamatta Bay, although their search was still continuing.

Following a precedent long sanctioned by supine magistrates and a compliant judiciary, Brady's seizure formally had nothing to do with the police investigation into the tattooed man's disappearance. The police simply did not have enough evidence on this score. Brady was taken into custody on a spurious forgery charge. It was a 'holding charge', one that the police had not proceeded with for lack of evidence; it had little prospect of ever being proved in the courts.

In accordance with another practice rarely challenged in the courts, the timing of the police raid had been made with a devious purpose in mind. With their patent neglect of civil liberties, the Australian judiciary, following English tradition, had set no firm limits on the amount of time a person could be subjected to police interrogation. The only requirement was that an accused person should be brought before a magistrate as soon as reasonably possible after their arrest. By seizing Brady in the early evening, when normal magistrates' hearings would not be held until the next day, the police gave themselves fifteen hours or more to question him, even if it meant he'd be interrogated for the whole night.

The detectives blatantly refused to tell Brady the cause of his arrest. When he inquired, Allmond replied that he 'would be told that later'. Whatever his personal feelings, the detective-sergeant was merely doing what he had been instructed to do in such circumstances. Brady was neither told of his rights nor given any opportunity to obtain legal advice. There was no formal requirement that he should be allowed these 'privileges'.

Grace Brady was distraught when the detectives barged in, and they offered her not a single word before completing the arrest of her husband. It was no accident that she was there during the raid. Against Allmond's protestations, Matthews had decreed that Grace would be a pawn in the police dealings with her husband. Prior had agreed, but with reservations, insisting that she was only to be involved if all else failed in securing Brady's co-operation.

Matthews planned that he and Allmond would stay with Grace at the flat for as long as they discreetly could, in the hope that she would be overwhelmed by the situation and accidentally let slip information about her husband's activities. Later, if she raised no strenuous objections, she would be conveyed to Central Street to give her husband the impression that she was under threat of being charged for assisting him to remain at large.

Matthews and Allmond remained in the flat with Grace Brady for an hour and more. They helped her to collect her husband's scattered belongings and made a specious, minute examination of the flat. While they 'worked' they attempted to prise information from her, talking disingenuously about Brady's tenancy of Cored Joy and his acquaintanceship with Reginald Holmes. To their chagrin Grace Brady did not respond. At first this was because she was dazed by her husband's arrest. But her Irish-Australian heritage then took hold, and she resisted the officers' blandishments stolidly.

Without legal justification, Matthews and Allmond then

took Grace to Central Street. An official statement later claimed that she had gone willingly. 'There is no use me staying here [at the flat] now,' she reportedly told the detectives, 'the people in the house will know about that [the police raid].' But Grace later denied saying any such thing. She said that she had been given no real choice about being ushered to a police car and driven to CIB headquarters. As she prepared to leave, Matthews stood to one side without helping her in any way. Allmond, by contrast, helped her gather up some groceries and other packages, and carried them for her to the waiting car.

Just after nine, almost three hours after the police raid, Grace Brady was placed in the care of a woman police officer, who took her to a room used by women police on the ground floor of the Central Street building. Grace took off her coat and hat, and the officer settled her in a comfortable chair with an electric radiator nearby. Over a cup of tea, the officer explained that Matthews and Allmond had hurried elsewhere in the building to interview the man Grace fondly called 'Pat'. The officer, with strict orders from Matthews, refused to tell Grace why her husband had been arrested, or why she couldn't be driven back to where she was staying.

For the moment, however, it seemed that the worst of her ordeal was over. She relaxed a little, and told the officer that she was pleased her eleven-year-old son was being kept clear of the family's troubles. She would have been dismayed if she had known that when she finally left Central Street the next morning, her frightened son would be holding one of her hands in the back of a police car.

Chapter 19

A TURBULENT DUEL

Patrick Brady was faced with overwhelming odds at CIB head-quarters, but the detectives knew he would not be easily intimidated. He was well aware that he was not required to make any admissions to the police. But he also understood that he could be mentally harassed for hours on end if he did not appear to co-operate with them. Besides, he always took an impish delight in matching his wits with his interrogators. Quite justly, he believed that he would not suffer violent physical intimidation. It was not part of the stock-in-trade used by Prior's CIB: in other parts of Australia at the time things were different, most particularly in Victoria. Brady's 'interview' with the police would be a psychological duel, with Superintendent Prior masterminding it until he left for home just before midnight.

On his arrival at Central Street, Brady was subjected to a process of 'softening up' that the police believed would help to put him in the right frame of mind. He was not taken to the normal interrogation rooms on the top floor of the Central Street building, but ushered into Prior's office to impress Brady with the gravity of the situation. Prior had deliberately left his hat and coat there so Brady might think that the

Superintendent himself was going to question him. But far from being intimidated, the two officers accompanying him found that the forger seemed to take this as a compliment.

Brady was left for over an hour in Prior's room to 'contemplate' his situation. The junior officers guarding him were told not to converse with him. He was supposed to become alienated, disoriented and malleable. But the police soon found that his enforced idleness had invigorated him, allowing him time to relax after the trauma of his arrest and prepare himself for questioning.

The interrogation began just after nine. Brady seemed to relish the first hour, sparring with Matthews and Allmond, upstaging their blandishments and threats with pithy quotations from literature. He mocked them as he refused to answer questions about his stay at Cored Joy or his relationship with Jim Smith. He was mute about any association with Reginald Holmes.

Progressively, however, Matthews became more intimidatory. Allmond faded into the background, as if he was alarmed by his colleague's manner. Matthews, cold-bloodedly, began to stack the deck for his trump card – a contrived meeting between Patrick Brady and his wife where it would appear that she was under arrest. He didn't mention Grace by name, made no explicit reference to her. But the implication was clear when he told Brady that his brother Peter could be charged for sending money to him via Alley's real estate agency at Cronulla under an assumed name.

Matthews knew he had struck decisively. Brady was immediately thrown off balance by the mention of his family. 'He appeared to be thinking,' one detective later recalled. Hesitantly, Brady acknowledged at last that he'd been at

Cronulla in early April. The official documentation recorded him as saying, 'I was living at a cottage at Cronulla, I took it from Alley.'

The detectives waited for him to say more, but Brady knew he had said enough to exonerate his brother, and soon became even more truculent than before. He refused point-blank to acknowledge that he had purchased the trunk and the mattress that had been delivered to Cored Joy, while admitting inconsequentially that he had sent the keys of the cottage back to Percival Alley with a bus driver.

Matthews and Allmond then made a theatrical exit, telling two officers standing by to remain on guard and not to talk to the suspect. Brady was left once more to ruminate, this time with the thought that members of his immediate family, including his wife, might be charged with criminal offences unless he co-operated more.

Matthews and Allmond conferred with Prior, who was preparing to leave for home. The Superintendent, like Allmond, was concerned that Grace Brady was being held in the building without her approval. He preferred, at least for the moment, to persist with methods of interrogation he knew and trusted best. Brady was left alone for over ninety minutes, with just one brief interruption. 'Good-day Paddy,' Prior said to him, as he went to his office to collect his hat and coat. Brady nodded back and replied, 'Good evening Mr Prior.'

Just after midnight, Allmond returned to the office in one last effort to cajole Brady. He waved away the junior officers and, like a confessor or confidante, took hold of a chair and moved it next to Brady's. The detective-sergeant told Brady that the police did not really believe he had killed Jim Smith. All they wanted, the detective whispered, was the real identity of the murderer. Brady recalled many years later that Allmond promised repeatedly 'he could walk straight out of the room' if he revealed what he knew about Jim Smith and Cored Joy.

Brady would have none of it. It was a serious misreading of his character to believe that he would. Allmond soon knew it was a stalemate, although he persisted with the forger for half an hour. At last he gave up and left the room, motioning the two junior officers outside to resume their silent vigil inside it.

Matthews now reckoned that he had a free hand with Brady. Prior had left, and Allmond had failed. Drama had turned to farce, with Brady already in custody for more than six hours. The official record of the following two hours is confused, and understandably so. What occurred reflected badly on the New South Wales police, and most of all on Detective-Sergeant Matthews. The crowning irony was that Brady emerged triumphant.

Between 12.30 and 1.30, in accordance with Matthews's orders that it should seem she was under arrest, Grace Brady was escorted into Prior's office by a woman police officer. Brady inquired, 'How are you dear?' Grace replied, 'All right.' A police officer later recalled Brady as then saying, 'This is a case of murder.' Grace fainted, falling in to the arms of Detective-Sergeant Allmond. A glass of water was summoned. Grace revived, and she reportedly told Brady to 'tell the truth about your visit to Cronulla' as she was led from Prior's room.

Both Bradys later remembered the occasion as one that had scarred them for life. Each had sincerely believed that Matthews was about to charge Grace with the commission of a criminal offence. One officer present was later prepared to admit that this bluff was Matthews's intent, despite official documentation suggesting that Grace's visit to Prior's room was a humanitarian gesture by the detective-sergeant to give Brady a few minutes with his wife.

Momentarily, in the grim early-morning atmosphere at Central Street, it appeared that Matthews succeeded. Within a few minutes of his wife's departure, Brady asked for pen and paper and prepared to write a statement.

Just after two o'clock, Matthews and Allmond watched anxiously as Brady completed a one page document. It was little enough, but Matthews anticipated that it would justify the planning and dubious tactics he had pursued to obtain it. To his dismay, however, Brady turned the tables on him. The small document did little more than acknowledge facts he could hardly deny. Faced with the evidence of his taxi ride with Bert McGowan, he admitted purchasing the mattress and the trunk, but made no effort to explain why. He admitted that Jim Smith was with him on the night of 8 April after the police presented him with the information they had received from Harry Levi and the Cecil's two regular customers. But his account of his last dealings with Jim Smith left the detectives flabbergasted.

As Brady told it, Jim Smith was still alive when he had walked to Charles Cooper's garage. He said that Jim Smith was the person he had been expecting to meet at the hotel at Tom Ugly's Point after he caught up with the taxi-driver at the bridge toll booth. He explained away his cab rides to Holmes's residence as having nothing to do with his stay at Cored Joy.

Beyond this, Brady simply refused to go. He knew he was under no legal obligation to provide incriminating information. If there were discrepancies between what he had written down and what the police knew, it was up to them to resolve them. In a case where it was likely there would be no direct, physical evidence, he would probably only have to give a reasonable explanation of his dealings with Jim Smith to walk from the court a free man.

The investigation seemed in tatters, but Matthews had no intention of releasing Brady from custody. At 2.30 Brady was led from Prior's room to be charged with the forgery offence. Soon after, he was led away to an ordinary cell nearby without being offered bail. Meanwhile, Grace Brady had made a brief formal statement to the police. She accounted for short visits she had made to Cored Joy, including the day she had been there when Percival Forbes had called in. She confirmed that she had visited her husband at three locations in North Sydney over the previous three weeks.

Allmond visited her before he left for home at about three. He apologised for intruding and inquired how she was faring. She seemed reasonably comfortable, and said she intended to stay at Central Street for the rest of the night.

Allmond left for his home in the suburbs after nineteen hours' continuous duty. He knew he would get little sleep. Matthews had arranged for a police car to collect him just before eight. He was to be a reluctant partner in a new devious plan his colleague had cooked up.

Chapter 20

THE CHARGE IS MURDER

Matthews and Allmond were affected next day by frustration, desperation and lack of sleep. They had gambled and failed in their bid for Brady's co-operation. By arresting him they had set the machinery of criminal justice in motion, putting themselves in a spot from where their options in continuing to deal with him became strictly limited. Once he was brought before a court on the 'holding charge', they no longer had the same control. He could be released by a magistrate and it would be difficult to keep him in custody unless he was publicly charged with involvement in Jim Smith's disappearance.

The detectives, understandably, still regarded Brady as the most obvious key to the success of their inquiries. Matthews in particular believed that, if the forger was pressured doggedly, he would finally crack. The menacing detective-sergeant was even prepared to gamble on charging Brady with the murder of Jim Smith in an attempt to coerce his collaboration. Prior and Allmond had their doubts. Brady had proved resilient under interrogation, despite his anguish over the treatment of his wife. His reputation as a man who would not 'shelf' anyone to the police had emerged untarnished from the late-night encounter.

More than Matthews, Prior and Allmond doubted whether Brady had actually killed Jim Smith, although they considered it probable he had been involved in the disposal of his body. Furthermore, while the law allowed considerable latitude to the police in their dealings with suspects like Brady, there were limits that could not lightly be ignored, although they might be manipulated for a time. Otherwise, the police might not only suffer public opprobrium, but find themselves on trial in court. Prior and Allmond had worried about such a fate when Grace Brady had been held at Central Street the night before.

The first sign of the detectives' desperation came five hours after Brady had been led away to a cell at Central Street. At 8 am, with a magistrate's hearing on the 'holding charge' only two hours away, a police car, Matthews and Allmond inside, pulled up outside the house where the Bradys' eleven-year-old son, John, was staying with his aunt. The boy was still in bed and Matthews ordered him to get dressed. John was then taken in custody to Central Street, while Matthews ensured that Brady knew his son was in the building. He hoped that the knowledge his son might be embroiled in court proceedings would intimidate the tough-minded prisoner.

Matthews reluctantly allowed Allmond to take John Brady to see his mother for a few minutes. He ran to her, and she kissed and hugged him. Allmond left them alone for a few minutes, ignoring his colleague's instructions. The boy was then led away to be interrogated by Matthews for over half an hour. Matthews took a statement from the boy and insisted that it be transcribed and typed up before John left. The detective towered beside the eleven-year-old as he signed it.

John Brady's statement linked his father more closely to

Jim Smith's visit to Cronulla. Whether it could ever be used in court was a question Matthews didn't care to contemplate for the time being. The statement confirmed that John was the person Johanna Molloy saw at the front gate on the morning Jim Smith was seen at Gladesville for the last time. Matthews regarded this as evidence that the missing man was 'lured' to Cronulla. Other detectives were not so sure. But it seemed beyond doubt that John Brady had carried a message to Smith from his father asking the boxer to meet him at the Cecil hotel that afternoon, and that the forger had sent money to pay the fare.

Whether by design or not, John Brady's presence at Central Street served another purpose for the detectives. He was returned to his mother not long before the magistrate's hearings for the day began in an adjoining building on Liverpool Street. Arrangements were made to convey mother and son home in a police car. So Grace was not present to proffer assistance to her husband when he was brought before the court.

Police made no mention of Jim Smith's disappearance at the hearing. Brady stood by stoically, knowing that if he played along he had a fair chance of securing bail on the forgery charge. He was deeply resentful that his son had been brought to Central Street. Rather than making him more amenable, it had given him more will to resist any further police demands made on him. The magistrate decided that he could be released on bail of three hundred pounds. But until this sum was raised, he had to return to his cell at the Central Police Station.

Unknown to Brady, as he was waiting to appear in court, Matthews and Allmond left Central Street on an urgent mission. They rushed to North Sydney to find Reginald Holmes, who had returned from Melbourne a few days earlier. Their plan was to confront Brady with the boatbuilder and put added pressure on him by giving him the impression that Holmes was 'ratting' on him. Holmes was at his boatyard when the police approached him shortly after ten. It almost seemed that he had been waiting for them, preparing for this encounter. He did not object to accompanying them to Central Street. Allmond told him to put on his coat. 'He did as he was told,' Allmond said later, 'he did not demur in any way.'

At CIB headquarters Holmes's compliance changed to anger when he was told of Brady's statement that he knew him. The haughty boatbuilder dismissed the claim as a lie. The detectives had Brady brought to the room where they were questioning Holmes. Pointing to the boatbuilder, Matthews asked Brady, 'Do you know this man?' 'That's Mr Holmes whom I mentioned in my statement,' Brady replied. The detectives assumed that Holmes would now acknowledge he knew Brady and that the scheme to convince Brady the boatbuilder was collaborating with the police would succeed. Matthews pointed to Brady and asked Holmes if he knew him. The boatbuilder looked at the forger carefully and said firmly: 'No, I do not know him.'

The interchange left the detectives nonplussed. Their situation worsened when word was brought that one of Brady's sisters was preparing to have her brother released on bail in less than an hour. They found a swift, if not quite legal response to this new crisis. Formally, Brady was now under the control of a magistrate's court, which had ordered his release if the money was found for bail. There were no other outstanding charges against him locally, and in the normal course he would be allowed to go free. But, as Brady's sister continued to make arrangements for his release, Matthews ordered a police car to be made immediately available.

The car set out with Brady squeezed in between Matthews and Allmond in the back seat. The journey initially retraced Brady's taxi ride with Bert McGowan. At each of the second-hand dealers where Brady had called, the officers reminded him of how his purchases of the mattress and the trunk implicated him in Jim Smith's disappearance. But if this disconcerted Brady, he didn't show it. He refused once again, as on the previous night, to explain his purchases. The police car was then directed on to Cored Joy, from where Matthews walked Brady to the shoreline of Gunnamatta Bay. He pointed to boats searching for the missing trunk. Far more optimistically than he really felt, the detective-sergeant said the trunk would soon be found. Brady seemed more bemused than anything else, commenting on the expense and indicating that he wondered what all the fuss was about.

There was one moment in the visit to Cored Joy when Brady appeared ready to become more forthcoming. In the shed at the rear of the cottage he looked down at the floor and said: 'There was a roll of canvas there,' and that it had belonged to Holmes. He then claimed he had telephoned the boatbuilder about it and had been instructed to take it by boat to the Port Hacking wharf, a remote spot on the southern shore of the waterway. He said he'd been told that 'there would be a man waiting for it'. Brady further recalled that he had believed it was equipment taken from a vessel called the *Pathfinder*.

Brady would say no more. He was enigmatic, and intentionally so. He refused to say whether he had carried out the boatbuilder's instructions. It was almost as if he was enjoying the game. Matthews became infuriated, although he tried not to show his anger. Allmond, on the other hand, acknowledged Brady's skill in attempting to implicate Holmes in events at Cored Joy without really letting on much.

On the journey back to Sydney the detectives made one final bid to win Brady's co-operation. The police car was directed to stop at the hotel at Tom Ugly's Point that Brady had visited two days after Jim Smith had last been seen. In the public bar, Matthews ordered a glass of port. Allmond, Brady and another detective preferred tots of rum. But this sudden touch of police conviviality did nothing to loosen the forger's tongue.

The detectives were tired and dispirited on their return to Central Street. Once Brady was led away, they were greeted with the news that his sister was sure to have him out on bail the next morning. The officers realised that they had reached a climactic moment. During the twenty-four hours since they'd apprehended Brady they had hardly advanced in solving the riddle of the Tiger shark and the tattooed arm. Next morning, at the very latest, their suspect would go free, placing their entire investigation in jeopardy. In what one of the officers later described as a 'throw of the dice', it was agreed that Matthews might be right – Brady would never come to the table with the police until he was charged with Jim Smith's murder.

At about 7.15 pm on Friday, 17 May 1935, Patrick Brady was led from a cell to the charge room at the Central Police Station and placed in front of Matthews. The detective-sergeant said: 'As a result of our inquiries we have decided to charge you with the murder of James Smith.' The formal charge was then read to him. It alleged that on or about 8 April he had feloniously killed Smith at Cronulla.

In most cases, this was a crowning moment for the police. For Matthews and Allmond the scene in the charge room this time was little more than a passing interlude, a break, before they started over again to see if there was any justification at all in claiming that Brady had killed Jim Smith.

Chapter 21

ROLLERCOASTER RIDE

By charging Patrick Brady with murder, the Sydney CIB had set the investigation on a course the police could not control. More and more, the detectives found themselves forced to concentrate their efforts on proving Brady was guilty, rather than seeking out alternative explanations. They had evidence enough that, whatever Brady had in fact done, it was unlikely he'd acted alone. But the only other person they'd discovered who might have been his accomplice was Reginald Holmes. Matthews and Allmond decided their best strategy for the moment was to play the two men off against each other.

Within minutes of Brady being charged the detective-sergeants were on the road again, despite less than five hours off duty in a day and a half. Their ploy was to surprise and shock Reginald Holmes into disclosing what he knew about the death of Jim Smith and the disposal of his body. Matthews hammered on the door of the boatbuilder's McMahon's Point residence, determined that Holmes would be one of the first to know Brady had been charged. He wanted Holmes to assume that, if he didn't co-operate, he would soon find himself in the same position.

The detectives confronted Holmes and his wife, Inie, in

their living room. Holmes showed flashes of hostility as he parried questions about his dealings with Patrick Brady and Jim Smith. He angrily denied knowing Brady, maintaining this claim even in the face of the evidence from the taxi-drivers about visits to McMahon's Point. He claimed that he had always been on good terms with Jim Smith. Inie Holmes followed her husband's line. She repeatedly denied ever meeting Brady. To the best of her knowledge, she said, the relationship between her husband and Jim Smith had always been amicable.

Matthews and Allmond left frustrated, but on their way back to Central Street they agreed that the visit had been worthwhile. The boatbuilder and his wife had finally seemed unnerved by the police questions, showing signs of real fear as the police had departed. The detectives decided to leave them simmering in the dark for a day or so.

Meanwhile, Patrick Brady was due to appear on the murder charge in the Central Police Court next morning. In the normal course, he would be remanded without bail to the Long Bay Gaol, where the detectives would have limited access to him. It was a Saturday, however, and Matthews and Allmond knew ways to keep the accused man at Central Street over the weekend.

After Brady was remanded he was returned to a cell at the Central Police Station, pending arrangements to send him to Long Bay. But these arrangements were simply not made. Matthews and Allmond determined to squeeze every possible advantage from the situation.

Within minutes of Brady's return to Central Street, his wife was ushered to him. It was not a social call. The Bradys were given no opportunity to talk privately. Once more the accused man was deliberately given the impression that Grace Brady was under threat of prosecution. After more than forty hours in custody, Brady appeared to be wilting. He warned his wife that she might be charged if she did not make a further statement to the police. She was then taken away and Brady was left in his cell alone for almost four hours. His reverie was broken in mid-afternoon when Allmond and another detective appeared at his cell door with a statement signed by Grace Brady. He read it over. If the officers thought it would put him off balance, they were wrong. There even seemed to be a hint of satisfaction in his voice as he handed the document back and said, 'That is right.'

The statement did no harm to Brady. Rather, it drew Reginald Holmes more closely into the investigation. The boatbuilder would have much to explain the next time he met with the police. From Grace Brady's statement it appeared that the boatbuilder had been bankrolling her husband through most of April until the middle of May. She revealed that her husband had received letters from the boatbuilder addressed to him under false names at various post offices. The sums had been sufficient to cover the rent at hideaways in North Sydney, with money left over.

After he read the document Brady was once more left alone in his cell. Allmond, as he left, said that it was now up to Brady to be more forthcoming with the police. The detectives waited anxiously to hear from their prisoner. Four hours went by and a little more. It was reported to the CIB that Brady ate a meal in his cell with 'studied leisure'. Just after seven, Brady sent a message to the detectives that he was prepared to make another statement.

Since mid-afternoon Brady had prepared for a virtuoso

performance. He sat down, ranged against Matthews, Allmond and two other detectives. A stenographer was ready to take down his remarks; the accused man knew that they could be used in evidence against him in court. He took command, allowing only occasional interruptions from his would-be inquisitors. He made it clear that if he was not permitted to speak as he wished, he would ask to be returned to his cell.

Under these circumstances, the police had no way of probing the truth of what Brady was saying. In the end, they decided it was probably a judicious blend of fact and fiction.

Brady reiterated, with a little more detail than previously, that Jim Smith did not die on 8 April or shortly thereafter. By his account, the missing man was still alive well into 9 April. He dictated to the police stenographer that on the night of 8 April, Smith left Cored Joy after two mysterious visitors called for him outside the waterfront cottage in the early evening. Before leaving to join them, Smith told Brady that one visitor was a friend of Reginald Holmes, but didn't identify the other. Brady did not see his friend for the rest of the night or the next morning, but Smith reappeared at Cored Joy later in the day after Brady returned from visiting Reginald Holmes. This was, he said, the last time he saw the missing man alive. Brady returned to Sydney in the afternoon by public transport. When he arrived back at Cronulla with Bert McGowan on 10 April, Smith was gone. Brady presumed, however, that Smith had been at Cored Joy the previous night. The forger said that he had discovered two empty beer bottles on the living-room table, with four unwashed glasses beside them.

The most remarkable parts of Brady's statement were yet to come. They concerned Reginald Holmes, and without explicitly saying so, Brady pointed to the boatbuilder as the man he regarded most likely to have been behind Jim Smith's disappearance.

Brady said his only involvement with Holmes had to do with a plot to defraud one of the boatbuilder's rich clients. He claimed that Holmes provided him with a cheque signed by this man, and that he learned to copy the signature in order to forge a cheque for a large sum that was later to be cashed. Brady explained that it was this deal that originally brought Holmes to Cored Joy.

Brady's account of events at Cored Joy placed Holmes at the waterfront cottage on the nights of 8 and 9 April – by any reckoning, that of the police or Brady, it was on one of these nights that Smith was seen alive for the last time. The accused man claimed that on 8 April, after Smith left, Holmes appeared at Cored Joy for discussions on the progress of the forgery. Brady said he then accompanied the boatbuilder back to the city and returned to Cronulla by bus at about eleven.

Brady told the police that after the discovery of Smith's arm he had confronted Holmes about his presence at Cored Joy on the night of 9 April. 'I know Mr Holmes was there,' Brady dictated in his statement. He said that Holmes had denied the arm was Smith's. The forger, by his own account, had then exclaimed disbelievingly: 'By Jesus, if this is him, that is done in that shack.' Holmes had then replied: 'Look, this is all wrong.'

Brady's account of Holmes's visits to Cronulla enabled him to explain away two of the clues that had led the police to regard him as a prime suspect. He said that his early morning taxi ride with Bill Brown had arisen when he found that Holmes had left a set of keys at Cored Joy after his visit on the night of 8 April. He hurried off to North Sydney to return them. The boatbuilder, according to Brady, was also responsible for his purchases of the mattress and the trunk. Holmes asked him to buy them and paid him five pounds to do it. The accused man explained that the items were bought to replace ones that had originally been on the *Pathfinder*, implying that they had been disposed of because they could have been used as proof of the fraud surrounding the sinking of the vessel.

There were discrepancies between what the accused man affirmed and evidence the police had gathered, and gaps in his review of events at Cored Joy. Brady failed to explain why he was responsible for arranging for Smith to go to Cronulla on 8 April, why he was so dishevelled on the morning after, why he hid his left hand in his overcoat pocket as if it was injured, why he seemed fearful of being followed in Bill Brown's cab.

Although Brady explained his purchases of the mattress and the trunk, he gave no indication of what had happened to the two mats that had been on the floor of a bedroom at Cored Joy, or why the walls of the room had been washed down. He did not tell why weights had gone missing from the shed at the rear of the waterfront cottage, nor the reason for the disappearance of the manilla rope and the killick from the motorised skiff he borrowed from the Smiths of Taloombi Street. He also refused to be drawn when the detectives asked what had happened to the brown leather bag he was seen carrying on two of his taxi rides.

Despite all this, the accused man's statement sent the detectives on a downward plunge on their rollercoaster, straight after they'd ridden high when he had emerged to make his second statement. Whether by design or not – and the detectives suspected Brady was astute enough to have worked out the police case from their earlier questioning – he had thrown several spanners in the works.

The detectives were very worried that Brady's statement made the charge of murder against him premature. They did not resile from their belief that he was embroiled in Jim Smith's disappearance, but were only too aware that his statement appeared to make out reasonably plausible explanations for most of his apparently suspicious activities.

It was almost midnight before Brady was led away to his cell. Briefly, before going home, Matthews and Allmond agreed that they must now make an all-out bid to force Holmes to reveal what he knew about the events at Cored Joy. The boatbuilder was hardly in a strong position to stall them any longer, given the accusations Brady had made against him in his second statement. The officers went their separate ways, agreeing to take Sunday off and meet again at eight on Monday morning to plan their tactics.

Chapter 22

BOATBUILDER AT BAY

Detective-Sergeant Matthews led off Monday's meeting by voicing his determination to bring pressure on Reginald Holmes and his wife. But the gathering was suddenly thrown into disarray by a message from the Water Police, who had their headquarters near Circular Quay. The boatbuilder was causing havoc at the wheel of a speedboat, weaving around ferries as they brought thousands of commuters to the city to begin their working day. Matthews and Allmond rushed to the waterfront to join one of three police vessels engaged in his pursuit. The detectives learned that it was a miracle Holmes was still alive.

Holmes's brother Leslie, who had joined in the chase, told the officers that the boatbuilder had attempted to commit suicide not long before. He had stopped his speedboat in Lavender Bay and, in full view of his brother and a group of spectators, had raised a pistol to his head and fired it. He'd toppled into the water, and everyone watching had thought he must be dead. But Leslie had noticed that, as he fell, one of Holmes's arms was caught by a trailing rope. His fall into the water had seemed to revive him, and he'd grasped at the rope, grabbed hold of it and scrambled back into the vessel.

Within seconds he'd started up the speedboat's engine again, and taken off with speed out of Lavender Bay to the mainstream of the harbour. Soon he'd been darting around vessels near Circular Quay, including the ferries.

Reginald Holmes then proved for the next four hours that he was a grand master of the environment he knew best. In one of the fastest speedboats in Australia, he led the police boats on a wild chase around Sydney Harbour, through Sydney Heads and into the open sea. He seemed several times to slow down to let one or other of the police vessels approach him. Then, with a touch on the speedboat's throttle and a quick turn of its wheel, he was off again, sometimes leading the police boats near rocky shoals, at other times turning sharply in circles.

The fastest police boat, the *Nemesis*, was forced to return to base for more fuel before it raced down the harbour again to where Holmes was hovering around near Watson's Bay, not far from the harbour's entrance. It seemed almost as if the North Sydney smuggler was waiting to continue a duel with the pride of the police fleet. As soon as the *Nemesis* was again in range, Holmes zipped off once more towards Sydney Heads. The two vessels plunged through the heavy swell at the harbour entrance, with two other police boats close behind. The race ended abruptly. About two kilometres into the Pacific Ocean, Holmes simply cut his engine and left the speedboat wallowing in the sea.

Matthews ordered the police helmsmen to approach the speedboat warily. They drew near, and Holmes stood up. It seemed for a moment or two that he was getting ready to plunge into the sea. As Matthews came within earshot, however, he heard Holmes say he needed bandages to bind a wound on his head. The police vessels approached the speed-boat from three sides. Holmes looked around and noticed Matthews. He shouted out, 'Why didn't you come to see me?' and went on: 'Jimmy Smith is dead and there is only another left.' He added: 'If you leave me until tonight I will finish him.'

In a moment or two the boatbuilder was unable to say any more. Leslie Holmes leapt into the speedboat, grabbed at his brother and pushed him into the well. Blood caked Holmes's forehead and stained his jacket. His hair was singed, there were dark streaks on his face – apparently powder burns – and a shallow wound gaped on his head. Leslie Holmes, assisted by the police, helped the wounded man into the *Nemesis*. Someone found a first-aid kit, applied antiseptic to his forehead and bandaged the wound. In a search of the speedboat, the police could find no sign of the weapon Holmes had used to try to kill himself. But they discovered the remains of a nickel-jacketed bullet, which, accidentally, it seemed, had missed penetrating Holmes's skull. Holmes reeked of brandy when he was brought on board the *Nemesis*. It seemed he had drunk a lot, as the police found an almost empty bottle in the bottom of the speedboat.

The *Nemesis* took over half an hour to make its way back to Circular Quay. The boatbuilder was still distraught, still at least partly drunk. He couldn't stop talking, at times incoherently, as the police boat made its way back along Sydney Harbour. Several times Holmes shouted that he was living in fear, claiming that the wellbeing of his whole family was being threatened. He yelled at Matthews: 'They say I have been squealing, but you know how much I have been doing that.'

Matthews ruthlessly decided to take advantage of the

situation. He ignored Holmes's need for treatment, and decided that the boatbuilder should be taken to Central Street, although Sydney Hospital was on the way from Circular Quay. Matthews later said that Holmes had asked to go to CIB headquarters, where he wished to clean up and change his clothes. It was a lame excuse and the detective-sergeant knew it.

Once more, however, Matthews's hopes were dashed. As Holmes sobered up he refused to elaborate on the remarks he had made earlier. He was belatedly conveyed to Sydney Hospital after half an hour of futile questioning. X-rays confirmed that the boatbuilder had experienced a near miss. The bullet had struck a bony section of his skull and splayed itself on his forehead, leaving the boatbuilder with only a superficial wound. Hospital doctors reported that his mental state was far worse. It was uncertain whether he had reconciled himself to the failure of his attempt at suicide. It was possible, doctors said, that he would try to kill himself again. Police and doctors agreed that he should remain in the hospital under observation, with relays of police on guard nearby.

Meanwhile, the police inquiries quickly lost momentum. As Holmes was jousting with the police on Sydney Harbour, Patrick Brady was again remanded on the murder charge and finally sent to Long Bay. Over the weekend he managed to arrange for legal representation at future court hearings, no thanks to the police. He only obtained representation when he spoke with a Salvation Army officer in his cell who carried a message to a firm of Sydney solicitors. His lawyer's advice was that he should refuse to give any further information to the CIB, and Brady intended to obey it.

At Sydney Hospital, Holmes's wound mended rapidly. But his mental condition remained unstable. The CIB was repeatedly refused permission to interview him. The junior detectives who guarded him reported that they had been unable to pick up any snippets of information from the boatbuilder.

Frustration mingled with determination at CIB headquarters. William Prior counselled Matthews and Allmond to be patient in their dealings with the boatbuilder. He was crucial to the police inquiries, particularly since Brady had made his second statement, but the legal admissibility of whatever he told them depended on his mental state.

Police were forced to concentrate their energies elsewhere. The hunt for the trunk in Gunnamatta Bay went on, but was now hampered by increasingly bad weather. Special efforts were made to check Brady's story about the dumping of the items he'd said had come from the *Pathfinder*. A police expedition to the location he'd mentioned did nothing to confirm it. At a lonely, isolated hotel near the Port Hacking wharf, an area surrounded by bush, the proprietor was certain that none of the items Brady had mentioned had been left there.

The officers puzzled over Holmes's remark that, since Smith was dead, 'there is only another left'. The boatbuilder had been unhinged at the time, and the police were not sure whether much store could be placed on the comment. Taken at face value, however, it might suggest that the boatbuilder had been subjected to blackmail, as the police were nearly certain he had been by Jim Smith. But they weren't sure who the boatbuilder had been referring to when he had said that, if he was permitted to remain free, he would 'finish him'. As Brady was in custody, and Jim Smith surely dead, he apparently wasn't referring to either of them.

Holmes remained under observation for several days. When he was finally released he was still fragile. His doctors warned that stress could precipitate a rapid deterioration in his condition, which would prevent him from being a credible witness in any court proceedings. Matthews and Allmond faced yet another disturbing challenge. The boatbuilder, and what he might tell them, were now just about the last hopes for the investigation.

Chapter 23

AN AFFAIR OF HONOUR

Reginald Holmes was released from Sydney Hospital three weeks before the scheduled start of the Sydney Coroner's first official hearing into the discovery of the tattooed arm. Matthews and Allmond found the time nerve-wracking. They met almost daily with the boatbuilder, who was often accompanied by his wife and sometimes by a legal adviser. If weather permitted, the detectives spoke with him on the roof of the Central Street police building, accompanied by the sights and sounds of Australia's busiest city.

At the direction of his doctors, the detectives treated Holmes with kid gloves. There were times when they could only stand by as he sat silently chain-smoking on a bench. Slowly the officers began to piece together Holmes's version of his dealings with Jim Smith and Patrick Brady – a catalogue of deception, blackmail and violent threats. Except for one occasion, the boatbuilder refused to permit what he said to be recorded formally. At times he insisted on speaking privately with Matthews.

Throughout the drawn-out interrogation, Holmes showed fear that his life was under threat. He spoke of phone calls to his home from people who did not identify themselves, warning that if he collaborated with the police he would be killed. It was this, he claimed, that had led him to deny knowing Brady. He said that he believed one of the most incessant callers was a man called Bampton, whom he had met in the company of Brady on several occasions. The boatbuilder said that Bampton was one of the accused man's brothers-in-law and had been involved with him in various scams. Other callers, he thought, were also associates of Brady.

Inie Holmes believed that her family was being terrorised. She said that on a number of occasions she had herself received threatening telephone calls when her husband wasn't home, and that she feared for her own life. She had taken precautions to ensure that the Holmeses' children were protected when they went to school and played with other children in the neighbourhood. Like her husband, she claimed that fears for her family's wellbeing had made her deny to the police that she had met Patrick Brady.

The police tried as best they could to ease these worries. They offered to place officers on twenty-four-hour guard in the Holmeses' home. But the boatbuilder and his wife rejected this, not least, he explained, because of the effect this might have on his children. Nor would Holmes accept a regular police guard outside his house. He said he was worried about what his neighbours might think.

At first Matthews and Allmond treated Holmes's remarks about his social position cynically, believing that the boatbuilder made them to attract their sympathy. But when he persisted in referring to the protection of his family's 'honour', they concluded he was really concerned about it. Matthews, in particular, regarded this as an exploitable weakness in the boatbuilder. He took him aside privately many times, warning that the boatbuilder's family would risk social ostracism if Holmes did not tell more about Jim Smith and Patrick Brady.

The detectives played a duplicitous game with Holmes. They skirted around his potential criminal liability, partly to avoid upsetting him, but also in a bid to gull him about his true standing in their inquiries. All of the detectives in the investigation believed that the boatbuilder had been suffi-ciently involved to be charged with criminal offences. Opinions varied: some thought he'd been merely an accomplice in the disposal of Smith's body, others that he might well have been the instigator of the missing man's murder.

By early June, with the Coroner's inquiry fast approach-ing, Matthews had no doubt that the police tactics had succeeded. He confided in Allmond that Holmes was 'singing nicely', even though the boatbuilder had only been prepared to sign one small statement, in the presence of his solicitor. In it, Holmes provided the police with a possible motive for Jim Smith's murder.

The boatbuilder's statement told how Jim Smith called at his former patron's home one Sunday afternoon, and despaired: 'This is a life and death matter.' Smith referred to the money he said Holmes owed him and went on: 'If I don't get the money they will shoot me.' The boatbuilder asked Smith who was threatening him and he replied: 'Brady and his friends.' Smith went on to explain: 'They blame me for putting the cops on to them over a cheque.'

Holmes's statement was corroborated by his wife. Inie declared that, not long after this alleged incident, Smith appeared at the family residence when her husband wasn't home. She said that Smith told her that 'he had been threatened that afternoon by two men'. 'He said a gun was pointed at his stomach,' she added.

In his private conversations with the police, the boatbuilder built on this with testimony that implicated Brady in Smith's disappearance and the disposal of his body. He acknowledged the accused man's visit to McMahon's Point on the morning of 9 April, when Brady had arrived in Bill Brown's taxi from Cronulla. To the detectives' surprise, he said that Brady had also made another visit that night. He admitted that Brady also visited him on other occasions in the weeks before Jim Smith disappeared.

As the boatbuilder slowly recalled his story, he sought to make himself out as more sinned against than sinning. This did not fit comfortably with what the police knew of his past. But it suited Matthews's purposes to tag him along for a while. Holmes seemed to live in a dream world where he could escape legal culpability for any involvement in Jim Smith's disappearance. This helped the police to obtain convincing testimony linking Brady with evil doings at Cored Joy.

Holmes claimed that he was blackmailed unmercifully by Jim Smith and, later, Patrick Brady. He said that Smith blackmailed him into financing his venture as proprietor of the Rozelle Athletic Club, and forced him to take him on as an employee. The boatbuilder admitted that after the sinking of the *Pathfinder*, he angrily resisted the missing man's demands to be paid for his role in the attempted fraud. In Brady's case, Holmes said that the accused man was fed information by Jim Smith. Brady spent time on the *Pathfinder* when Smith was preparing it for scuttling, and gathered information he used for blackmail.

Holmes would not admit it, but it seemed to Matthews and Allmond that Brady's recent dealings with the boat-builder probably had nothing to do with Jim Smith. They thought it most likely that, as a result of blackmail or not, the two men had joined in a forgery enterprise, probably involving one of the boatbuilder's customers.

Holmes said that Brady's blackmailing began on the morning of 9 April after the accused man was dropped at McMahon's Point by Bill Brown. The boatbuilder said that he gave Brady money for his fares to and from Cronulla and other expenses, including his third week's rent at Cored Joy. After Brady's visit at about eight the same day, he provided additional sums.

For the police, however, Holmes's testimony of his meeting with Brady on the night of 9 April began to emerge as a dramatic turning point in their inquiry. At first Holmes only spoke fitfully about it. But gradually he told of a macabre confrontation with Brady at the boatbuilder's residence, linking Brady indisputably with the death of Jim Smith and the disposal of his body.

Chapter 24

A WANDERING ARM

Reginald Holmes described his meeting with Patrick Brady on the night of 9 April as the most frightening experience of his life. He told the detectives that the accused man arrived unannounced at Lower Bay View Street at about 8 pm and barged his way into the house, carrying a leather kitbag. The boatbuilder took him to his study, where Brady straightaway unclipped the leather bag. He pulled out Jim Smith's tattooed arm, held it up in front of Holmes, and told the boatbuilder that he would suffer the same fate as his former employee if he did not co-operate in helping to remove all traces of Jim Smith's murder at Cored Joy, not least by giving the forger money.

More than twenty years later Leonard Allmond still vividly recalled several times when Holmes had spoken of this event. Allmond said that 'Holmes when interviewed went so far as to to say Brady arrived at his home with the bag' and that 'he opened the bag and produced Smith's arm'. Another detective present on some of these occasions was Detective-Constable 'Danny' Calman, who, twenty years later, as the Superintendent in charge of the Sydney CIB, also remembered Holmes describing the meeting in the same way. But Calman went further, saying that the boatbuilder claimed to have learned from Brady what he later did with the arm. 'It is beyond doubt,' Calman said, 'the arm was thrown into the sea at Maroubra.'

Inie Holmes told the police that her husband suffered deep shock in the wake of Brady's visit. Although she was not present when the accused man was said to have produced the arm, she recalled him carrying the kitbag as he forced his way into their residence. She described how her husband was distraught after Brady left, and said that he warned her that the forger was threatening to harm everyone in the family. Later, she said, when Holmes began to regain some composure, he told her what had happened in his study. She said it was the first time she had realised the depth of her husband's involvement in crime and how it might threaten her sheltered existence.

The detectives first regarded Holmes's story with disbelief. Could Brady have really carried Jim Smith's severed arm from Cronulla to McMahon's Point and then on to Maroubra? But as the slow interrogation of the boatbuilder went on, they decided that he was not playing make-believe. At any mention of the meeting Holmes became so obviously stressed that the questioning sometimes had to be terminated. More significantly, the detectives found that Holmes's account of his dealings with Brady fitted with many of the facts they had been able to gather on Jim Smith's disappearance.

The boatbuilder said that he first learned the accused man was in a serious predicament after his arrival at McMahon's Point in Bill Brown's taxi. Brady, who seemed close to despair, referred to Jim Smith's death without stating precisely what had happened, and demanded money to help him deal with the situation. Holmes, reluctantly, gathered all the spare cash he could find and gave it to him. But he warned that he was not prepared to give Brady any more. It was this warning, so the boatbuilder said he believed, that led Brady to return that night with Smith's arm.

Holmes told police that after he was threatened with the severed limb, Brady had gone on to describe the arrangements made to remove all traces of Smith's death at Cored Joy. Holmes said the forger told him that the remainder of Smith's body was dumped in Forbes's trunk in Gunnamatta Bay, together with the Scotch rug and the two mats that were missing from the waterfront cottage. Brady claimed that the kapok mattress was also destroyed.

According to Holmes, he was not a witness to any of these events. What he told the police was no more than hearsay – there was no legal proof that they had actually occurred. Nevertheless, it was a strong indication to Matthews and Allmond that their earlier speculation about the events at Cored Joy was on the right track.

The detectives, however, were still puzzled about the extent of Holmes's involvement in the death of Jim Smith and the disposal of his body. Holmes consistently denied Brady's claims that he had visited Cored Joy. He refused to countenance the suggestion that he was the person the accused man had been planning to meet when he set out in Bert McGowan's taxi the morning after his visit to McMahon's Point on the night of 9 April. The boatbuilder ignored requests to explain what he had been doing on the afternoon of 10 April, after Brady had returned to Cronulla with McGowan, despite testimony from some of his employees that he had left McMahon's Point without giving any explanation for his absence.

In a bid to break this impasse, Matthews and Allmond cajoled Holmes into accompanying them to Cronulla for a visit to Cored Joy. They showed him over the waterfront cottage, and spent time with him in the shed behind it. He continued to deny ever being there. But the detectives had set a cunning trap and believed the boatbuilder's reactions showed that he was lying. As the police walked Holmes around the premises, they deferentially allowed him to lead the way. They found that the boatbuilder seemed curiously familiar with the cottage as he led the detectives from one room to another and into the shed outside.

This episode provided no legal proof that Holmes had previously visited Cored Joy. But it left the detectives suspicious that the boatbuilder had at best only told half-truths about his relationship with Brady, maintaining a cagey silence about the depth of his involvement in the mystery of the tattooed arm.

For the time being, the officers decided that this was a factor they must ignore. Matthews emphasised that, with the opening of the Coroner's inquiry only days away, their task was to ensure that the Coroner was presented with enough evidence to put Brady on trial for Smith's murder. If this meant that Holmes's culpability went unexamined, so be it. They could not lose their star witness.

Chapter 25

CORONARY

The members of the task force gathered at Central Street on the day before the opening of the Coroner's inquiry to review the evidence against Patrick Brady. Without the discovery of the rest of Jim Smith's body, there was still nothing to show how he had actually died. But the officers believed that they had gathered evidence enough to convince the Coroner to put Brady on trial for murder. Even if he had not actually killed Smith, he could still be equally liable under criminal law if it was shown that he had known about, and participated in, the events that had led to Smith's death and the disposal of his body.

The foundation of the case against Brady was testimony confirming his presence in the vicinity of Cored Joy on 8 April and the opportunity this had given him to be involved in Jim Smith's disappearance. The case rested partly on the evidence of those who had seen Brady and Smith at the Cecil hotel at that time. It was reinforced by the evidence of the Cronulla garage proprietor, Charles Cooper, and his taxi-driver, Bill Brown, who suggested that Brady had remained in the area overnight.

To add to this was the testimony of the three witnesses

who had seen Brady at Cronulla on the morning of 9 April. Each suspected that Brady had been involved in some funny business. The witnesses explained that Brady had appeared dishevelled and distraught. Each was given a patently untrue reason for Brady's early morning journey to Sydney. As well as this, his fellow passenger on the cab ride to Sydney claimed that Brady had been hiding an injured hand.

By itself, as the detectives acknowledged to each other, this evidence was hardly sufficient to show that Brady had actually killed Jim Smith. But as Matthews stressed, and the other officers agreed, the prosecution case would be transformed if Reginald Holmes would reveal to the Coroner the details of his meeting with Brady on the evening of 9 April. Unless Brady could rebut this evidence there was a fair chance he would be placed on trial for murder.

Matthews explained to his colleagues that Holmes's testimony about his night meeting with Brady on 9 April, and his description of what had followed in its wake, could serve another purpose. Combined with Bert McGowan's evidence about the accused man's purchases of the trunk and the kapok mattress and their delivery to Cored Joy, and the corroborative testimony of the second-hand dealers who had sold these items, Holmes's testimony – if he would give it – should be sufficient to secure Brady's conviction for being an accessory to murder, even if it would not prove he was responsible for killing Smith.

On the afternoon before the Coroner's inquiry, Holmes paid a visit to Central Street to meet Matthews. The detective-sergeant privately discussed the police case with him. Matthews, triumphantly, told Allmond afterwards that the boatbuilder was in reasonably good spirits. Holmes seemed resigned to his role as star police witness, and prepared to reveal the details of his dealings with Patrick Brady, including the meeting where the accused man had brandished Jim Smith's severed arm. The detective-sergeant was smiling, for once.

Chapter 26

MURDER IN TAIL-LIGHT ALLEY

The Sydney Harbour Bridge was opened in 1932. It brought many changes to the city. At the southern end of the bridge, for instance, the vehicular ferries that used to run to and fro across the harbour from Dawes Point ceased operation, and the area became a quiet haven at night, disturbed only by the dull background noise of the bridge traffic overhead.

Hickson Road, which skirted the harbour at Dawes Point, was transformed beneath the bridge into what was popularly known as a 'tail-light alley', a trysting place for lovers in cars. Patrolling police mainly turned a blind eye to the activities they officially described as 'petting parties'.

Just before 9 pm on 11 June 1935, the evening before the opening of the Coroner's inquest, Sergeant Percy Thornber of The Rocks Police Station set out on foot to patrol the area that included Dawes Point. He enjoyed the break from routine duties – it was a pleasant night, with just a hint of mist on the harbour. He studiously ignored a number of vehicles parked with their lights doused.

Under the bridge at Dawes Point, the sergeant's curiosity was aroused by a car parked unusually with its headlights blazing. He would have given it no more than a glance except that, as he came within the beam of its headlights, a man got out of the automobile, walked across the road, and joined another man, who was leaning over an iron railing, looking at the harbour below. More surprisingly, the car started up and passed him at a fast pace. He wasn't able to catch the number on its licence plates, but he recognised it as a Nash sedan and noticed it had a spare wheel attached at its rear between two bumperettes. After the vehicle sped away, he saw the two men close to the water walk off in the same direction.

At about the same time, a workman named Jack Thomas was staring out of the window of his rented room in one of the squalid tenements that lined the streets of The Rocks. He had a clear view of Hickson Road after it emerged from under the bridge in the direction the Nash had gone. Just after nine, Thomas later recalled, he saw a car parked on Hickson Road. Its headlights were dimmed. The front door beside the kerb was open. A man was standing near it. As Thomas watched, he heard two or three sharp noises coming from the direction of the automobile. For a moment or two, the man beside it seemed to stand still, then he bent over, straightened, and walked up Hickson Road in the direction of Dawes Point, where he disappeared from Thomas's view.

Jack Thomas went to bed soon after. Before he retired, however, he noted that the car was still parked on Hickson Road, headlights burning. Thomas decided not to report the incident to the authorities. He had lived in The Rocks for ten years, and knew that collaboration with the police was not a local custom.

Jack Wynne also lived close by. Whenever he could, Jack went fishing from one of the wharves on the other side of Hickson Road. He spent most of the early evening of 11 June on a wharf not far from Dawes Point. He later remembered that he hadn't caught much. He started fishing just after 5.30 pm, and he stayed longer than planned in the hope his luck would change. At about nine he heard noises like gunshots coming from the direction of Hickson Road. Like his neighbour, he regarded this as none of his business. After fishing for about another half-hour, Wynne began to make his way home. As he was approaching the Hickson Steps stairway, which led from Hickson Road up a steep cliff to part of The Rocks above, he saw a dark sedan parked nearby, with its headlights on. At the steps he saw a man he didn't know. He brushed past him quickly without a word and went home to bed.

Just after midnight two uniformed constables drove along Hickson Road. Near Hickson Steps the officers saw the sedan. Its dimmed headlights were still burning, and its kerb-side door remained open. One of the constables went to investigate. As he approached the sedan, he saw a man behind the steering wheel with his head sagging. He thought the man was ill, and called to his companion for help. A few moments later the other constable leaned through the open door of the vehicle. He felt the head of the man behind the steering wheel. 'He's dead,' he called out.

The police car was not equipped with radio. One officer remained on guard, and the other went to The Rocks Police Station to telephone for a mobile CIB unit with two-way radio communication. It arrived at Hickson Road at about 1.30 am. The detective-sergeant who arrived in it peered into the Nash in the pale light of electric torches. He saw that the eyes of the dead man were closed and that his spectacles were firmly in place. There were no signs of a violent struggle. A hat was still resting on the back of the deceased man's head, and the body was firmly set behind the steering wheel. The dead man's legs remained in the driving position, while the hands were resting on his thighs, as if he was still alive. The detective-sergeant eased himself into the sedan's front seat. He undid the dead man's coat and found bloodstains on his shirt and singlet. He then discovered three gunshot wounds puncturing the upper left side of his chest.

Because of the positioning of the body, the junior officers thought that the man had committed suicide. A quick visual examination of the vehicle seemed to confirm this. They found the shell of one bullet below the front seat, and two others on the floor at the rear. But they couldn't find a gun in the car, nor in the surrounding area. This was, the detective-sergeant concluded, a case of murder. He searched the coat of the deceased man, and found a driving licence. He checked with police headquarters and found that the vehicle was registered in the same person's name as the one on the licence.

Within minutes the detective-sergeant sent officers rushing to the homes of Matthews and Allmond. By 2.30 they had joined the gathering near Hickson Steps, as had Dr Aubrey Palmer, the Government Medical Officer. Matthews and Allmond took it in turns to examine the body in the automobile. It took just a glance from each to make a positive identification. The dead man in the car was Reginald Holmes.

The two officers stood beside the Nash sedan for a minute or two without saying anything, then commandeered a police car and set out grimly for North Sydney just after three.

The only house still lit up in Lower Bay View Street was the Holmeses' residence. The detectives were ushered into the main living room. Five people were there, with unfinished drinks scattered around, as if Inie Holmes and her guests were taking part in a wake. The group included Albert Stannard, who was a launch proprietor and close friend of the deceased, his wife, Holmes's brother Leslie, and another male friend of the family. Their first moments of anguish seemed to have passed already, and they showed little surprise when Matthews announced that Reginald Holmes was dead.

Inie Holmes explained that her husband had left home a little after 8 pm. She hadn't seen him since. When he'd left she'd believed that he was in serious trouble. She'd called in people to stay with her because she'd had a premonition he wouldn't return alive.

The detectives realised that there was no useful purpose to be served by intruding on such obvious grief. Within minutes of their arrival at Lower Bay View Street, they were driving back to the murder scene near the Hickson Steps, where Dr Palmer had made a preliminary examination of Holmes's body. An officer from Central Street had begun searching for fingerprints on the Nash sedan, and had collected the bullet shells in the vehicle for ballistic examination.

By six in the morning, curious passers-by were joining the police for a minute or two, mainly waterside workers going to the nearby wharves. Small groups of residents looked down at the Nash sedan from the Hickson Steps. The noise of early morning traffic was building up above on the harbour bridge. The night shadows were beginning to mingle with the approaching dawn. The lovers had long since gone. After Holmes's body was taken away, Allmond took charge of the Nash sedan. He slid behind the steering wheel and started up the engine to drive it to Central Street, where it was to be further examined.

Allmond, many years later, mused that his lone journey to Central Street in Holmes's car was one of the strangest experiences of his life. Fate, or whatever you might call it, he reminisced, had played the leading role in bringing about the accidental discovery of Jim Smith's tattooed arm. Fate had now intruded once again, making it highly unlikely there would ever be an official explanation for the death of Jim Smith.

Chapter 27

A FATAL DOMINO

In the game of dominoes the loss of one piece can lead to others being quickly surrendered. The murder of Reginald Holmes was a deadly domino for the police investigation. The North Sydney boatbuilder was the only person the police had found who could provide the evidence necessary to link Patrick Brady closely to Jim Smith's disappearance. Matthews and Allmond made desperate efforts to resurrect their case against the accused man. But from the outset, they suspected they were playing a losing game.

The search for the trunk finally had to be abandoned. In a last, all-out bid, Allmond and other officers made flights in RAAF planes, sweeping across Gunnamatta Bay, with divers waiting to search the bed of the bay. Allmond long remembered one time when he believed he had finally spied the missing trunk, standing out as a dark shadow in the water about half a kilometre south of Cored Joy. But the marker he'd thrown from a plane to designate the spot had floated away before a diver could get to it. On another flight soon after he'd been unable to locate the spot. Others fared no better.

The detectives turned to Inie Holmes, in the hope that she might be able to provide testimony that could partly substitute for her husband's evidence. Despite her grief, she agreed to co-operate with the police as best she could. She was under twenty-four-hour police guard as she prepared for her appearance as a witness at the Coroner's inquiry, which began on schedule despite Holmes's murder. She appeared mournfully at the Coroner's Court, on the edge of The Rocks district, roughly a kilometre from where the boatbuilder had died. Within minutes, she was at the centre of a legal storm.

It is an axiom of Australian criminal law that testimony called 'hearsay' is not ordinarily allowed to be used against an accused person. It is 'second-hand' knowledge: knowledge possessed by a person describing events relayed to them by someone else. The police sought to have Inie Holmes give evidence like this at the Coroner's hearing. She was to describe activities she only knew about because her late husband had spoken to her about them. By a strange loophole, to do with the ancient English origins of the coronial office in New South Wales, hearsay evidence could be admissible at a Coroner's inquest. It was a gap in the law the detectives set out to exploit as best they could. Their reasons would have appealed to Machiavelli.

The officers knew that any hearsay evidence Inie Holmes was allowed to present to the Coroner could not later be used in any criminal proceedings. For the time being, however, it could be used to enable the Coroner to exercise his authority to commit Brady for trial on the charge of murder in the Supreme Court of New South Wales. Meanwhile, the officers hoped, they would win time to search for new evidence against the accused man.

The detectives also knew that Inie Holmes's testimony would be widely reported in Sydney's newspapers. It was a prospect they anticipated with satisfaction. Even if the evidence she gave before the Coroner could not be used later, it would be read by many potential jurors. They might remember it, even if they were supposed to shut it out of their minds, persuading them to reach a verdict of guilty in the case of Patrick Brady.

From the moment Inie Holmes appeared in the witness box, a tough forensic duel erupted between the Coroner and Clive Evatt, a rising Sydney barrister who had been briefed to appear for Brady by his solicitors. Evatt declared that the admission in evidence of information relayed by her husband to Inie Holmes would be outrageous. It offended, he observed, every rule of evidence normally applied in court proceedings. The Coroner, however, peremptorily rejected the barrister's submissions. Within hours, Inie Holmes's evidence was head-line news.

Even Sydney's most conservative newspaper, the *Sydney Morning Herald*, reported next morning that Inie had made 'dreadful allegations' about Patrick Brady. She was permitted to testify publicly that her late husband had 'told me that Brady had murdered Smith', and that Holmes had said that Brady had put Jim Smith's body 'in a tin trunk, took it out in a boat, and put it overboard'.

At Central Street, Matthews and Allmond felt that the Coroner was helping them to make the best of a tough case. At the Coroner's Court, Clive Evatt was alarmed. He moved to halt the proceedings. Before a judge of the State Supreme Court, the barrister turned the tables on the Coroner, using ancient precedent to his client's advantage.

The Coroner, Evatt told the judge, was not permitted to run an inquest into a man's death when all he possessed of the missing man's torso was his tattooed arm. The barrister claimed that a Coroner only had authority to investigate an unexplained death when most of a person's body was in his legal possession. The reason for this stemmed from ancient English law, which required proof that Smith had died within the geographical area under the Sydney Coroner's jurisdiction. If other parts of Smith's body were found in a different area, another Coroner would also have the power to inquire into the death, perhaps with a different result. The judge agreed and stopped the Coroner's proceedings forthwith.

Evatt's victory did not halt proceedings against Brady altogether. In the wake of the judge's decision, official arrangements were made for a new hearing before a magistrate, who could still decide that the accused man should be arraigned before the Supreme Court. This time, however, hearsay testimony could not be admitted. One of the few ways Inie Holmes was now able to point to Brady's possible guilt was to agree that, on his early morning visit to McMahon's Point on 9 April, she'd noticed a cut on the forger's right hand, with blood around it.

Matthews and Allmond were heartened a little when the magistrate decided Brady should be placed on trial. But their optimism was short-lived. Without the evidence from Reginald Holmes, the prosecution case against Brady withered and died. For a day and a half the accused man was on trial in the dock at the Central Criminal Court at Darlinghurst before Sir Frederick Jordan, the Chief Justice of New South Wales. Once the prosecution evidence had been delivered, the Chief Justice ruled it too weak to require Brady even to make out a defence. He ordered that the jury should acquit him forthwith.

The police case against Patrick Brady was at an end.

His acquittal meant that he could never again be charged with the murder of Jim Smith. Nor could he be charged with offences closely related to his death or the disposal of his body. Three gunshots near Sydney Harbour Bridge just after 9 pm on 11 June 1935 had guaranteed that Brady would suffer no legal stain.

For Prior, Matthews, Allmond, and the other detectives, this was a dismal moment. They had endured more than two months of incessant activity, battling fatigue, being forced to make decisions on the run, with little time to pause and reflect on what they were doing. Even Matthews would later grudgingly admit that the hurried decision to charge Patrick Brady in an attempt to make him co-operate had backfired disastrously. The detectives had underestimated his resourcefulness and resilience. By charging him with murder the CIB had been forced to neglect clues indicating that Brady was not necessarily the person who had actually killed Jim Smith, although the detectives had no doubt he knew much about it.

The death of Reginald Holmes weighed heavily with Frank Matthews. He was the one who had convinced Superintendent Prior to agree not to place the boatbuilder under constant police guard. The detective-sergeant had argued that Holmes, in his fragile state, might otherwise stop collaborating with the CIB.

Prior did not engage in recriminations. He regarded Holmes's death as part of the give and take of police work. He emphasised that if anyone bore the ultimate responsibility for the failure of the police case, it was him. His colleagues noticed that he later showed more than a hint of respect for the man he always called 'Paddy'. They believed he had admired Brady's tenacity in resisting police threats and blandishments. Brady, too, many years later, remembered his dealings with Prior with a touch of affection. He said that the man he had dutifully called 'Mr Prior' had, unlike Detective-Sergeant Matthews, always been 'fair' towards him.

But there was still another twist in the tale of the shark arm murders.

Chapter 28

MURDER BY REQUEST

By 1935 the names of Al Capone and other American gangsters were almost as well known in Australia as in their own country. Their exploits, depicted in Hollywood movies, had brought new 'angles' to the reporting of local crime, as well as American words and phrases. To some Sydney newspapers Reginald Holmes's death was a 'gangland killing'. One paper declared that the boatbuilder had been 'taken for a ride'. Another reported that 'Chicago methods' had been employed to bring about the boatbuilder's death. These reports were no more than journalistic fantasies.

After his last meeting at Central Street with Matthews, Holmes went on to a meeting with his legal advisers. His family later told the police that he came back shattered. He had learned that his appearance as a witness before the Coroner threatened him far more than he had realised. At best, he was told, his admissions of criminal associations with Brady and Smith would make him a pariah in the upper reaches of local society. He would be expelled from the Royal Sydney Yacht Club. Worse still, Holmes's lawyers explained, there was every chance he would be prosecuted for his part in the events surrounding Jim Smith's death. He had almost certainly broken the law when he'd not reported to the police that Brady had told him Smith had been murdered. More seriously, he had given Brady money to help him dispose of Jim Smith's body, making him potentially liable as an accessory to murder.

An unsigned note in the police records pointed to what followed. It was a statement Inie Holmes gave to a detective at her home, shortly after her husband's death. In forty-seven words it said that: 'Mrs Holmes is of the opinion that the deceased left his home on the night of the murder to keep an appointment with some person and intended in some way or other to meet his death in a manner which would not bring disgrace to his family.'

This information explained why the deceased man's body had been positioned so naturally behind the wheel of his car. The boatbuilder had simply waited to be shot, with his eyes tightly closed. It also explained to Matthews and Allmond why Inie Holmes and the others they had met at McMahon's Point after finding his body had shown no real surprise when told of his death.

A quick check with his bank disclosed that the boatbuilder had withdrawn a large amount of cash even before his visit to his solicitors. It had not been discovered on his body. Inie Holmes and the dead boatbuilder's closest associates claimed to have no knowledge of it. The money was easily enough, the detectives knew, for Holmes to have hired the services of a gunman.

The detectives probed the boatbuilder's personal business and discovered another reason why Holmes would wish to stage his own murder rather than commit suicide. He had purchased very lucrative life insurance policies, which provided that no payments would be made if he took his own life. The boatbuilder probably had not been aware of this when he had tried to do away with himself in May. Since then, however, as the police learned from Inie Holmes, the legal situation had been explained to him.

Some of the CIB's most conclusive evidence that Holmes had engineered his own murder came from Prior's army of fizgigs. The Superintendent pulled out all stops to discover Holmes's killer. He spent hours meeting informers, and put the word out to seek and send information. More than twenty years later, well after the Superintendent had retired from the police force, cryptic notes from fizgigs about Holmes's murder still sat in the archives of the New South Wales police.

Prior's informers confirmed that the boatbuilder had acted through an intermediary to buy the services of a hitman, probably late on the afternoon before the opening of the Coroner's inquest. The boatbuilder, it seemed, had not wanted to come face to face with the man who was to kill him. One fizgig, who urged Prior to destroy his note after he read it, named two men with long criminal records, saying that they had acted together to carry out the contract. He then described how they had set up an alibi for themselves with the proprietor of a rooming house at The Rocks.

Other informers also mentioned other men. But only one of the alleged killers, a waterfront identity named Jack Strong, was charged with committing murder, after his fingerprints were found on the chassis of the boatbuilder's Nash sedan.

Strong was not the only man put in the dock of the Central Criminal Court for Holmes's murder. Beside him at Darlinghurst in November 1935 stood one of the late boat-builder's closest friends, Albert Stannard, the launch owner who was at Holmes's house when Matthews and Allmond came to report his death. Strong had occasionally worked for Stannard.

At a hearing that led to the committal for trial of the two men on the murder charge, no mention was made of other men some of the fizgigs had suggested had murdered Holmes. Nor was the reference made to them in any later court proceedings. Instead, the official scenario was that Strong and Stannard had cold-bloodedly conspired to murder Holmes.

The case against Stannard largely relied on the evidence of Sergeant Percy Thornber of The Rocks Police Station, and a man called Oliver Summers. Although he wasn't entirely sure, Thornber said that Stannard could have been the person he had seen getting out of Holmes's car near Dawes Point. He had known the launch proprietor for about nineteen years and the man, he said, appeared to be of the same height and build.

Summers was a chiropodist who lived at a hotel near Circular Quay. He claimed that he had been walking down the Hickson Steps at about nine, and had almost reached the bottom when he'd heard three gunshots. He had seen a man below walking past the steps on Hickson Road. The man had turned his head over his left shoulder, and Summers had seen him straight in the face in the light of a nearby street lamp. He said he'd later recognised the man as Albert Stannard.

The case against Strong relied on the fingerprints found above the left front door on the chassis of Holmes's Nash sedan. There were four prints of a left middle finger. This was consistent, the prosecution argued, with the accused man standing at the open car door as he initially steadied himself and then convulsively moved three times as he shot Holmes from point-blank range.

Stannard's defence was that he had been at a cinema with his wife, Enid, at the time Holmes had been killed. Strong admitted seeing the boatbuilder on the day he was murdered, but in entirely different circumstances from those the prosecution alleged. He said that he'd accidentally met Holmes in the late afternoon when the boatbuilder had almost run him down in his car. He told the court that he had called out to the driver: 'Where the bloody hell are you going; it is bastards like you that kill people.' Then he'd recognised Holmes, whom he had known casually for about two years. Holmes had offered him a lift, which he'd accepted, even though he'd only been travelling 100 yards to a nearby hotel. This, Strong claimed, was why his fingerprints were left on the vehicle.

The jury went out and, after deliberating for twenty hours, failed to reach a verdict. Less than a month later the men were back in the dock on the same charge. On the fourth day the jury intervened, informing the court that the evidence suggesting that Stannard was near Hickson Steps when Holmes was killed was 'not satisfactory'. The jurors also said that the prosecution had not rebutted the launch proprietor's alibi. The jury found him not guilty and he was set free. The trial of Strong continued for a further day and a half, until the jury acquitted him as well.

The CIB dropped investigations, and no one was ever again brought to trial for the murder of Reginald Holmes.

Chapter 29

SHADOW OF SUSPICION

After Brady's acquittal, many still believed that he was responsible for Smith's murder. Some, Brady learned, said that it was only the murder of Holmes that had saved him from the gallows or life imprisonment. The shadow of suspicion followed him for years. 'Whenever I walk into a hotel bar or a room where there are a few other people, I can feel the atmosphere,' he said towards the end of his life. People whispered 'that's Patrick Brady', and he knew that they were referring to him as a murderer.

Brady denied constantly that he had killed Jim Smith. In 1963 he said: 'As I was acquitted of the charge of murdering Jim Smith by direction of the judge, that means I can't be charged again with the murder, even if I was to say I was guilty of it.' But he went on: 'With my dying breath, I'll repeat, I didn't do it.' Later he re-affirmed: 'I had nothing to do with Jim Smith's death.' His pleas of innocence mostly fell on deaf ears. But there are strong reasons to believe that he was telling the truth.

Brady, as his official record demonstrated, was a criminal of guile, not violence. He never carried knives or guns. It made him an unlikely suspect if Smith was killed by a lethal weapon.

Almost from the beginning of the official inquiries into

Smith's disappearance, however, the possibility that he died by gunshot or knife attack was glossed over or ignored. This was despite the fact that Detective Head, who was well experienced in dealing with violent crime, had noted 'wounds' on the tattooed arm that he thought had been made by a dangerous weapon.

At the Coroner's office, the medical experts had barely touched on this issue. The Government Medical Officer, Dr Aubrey Palmer, had suggested in passing that at least one 'wound' could have been caused by a bullet, because of ragged tissue around it. Most of his attention, however, had been directed at satisfying the Coroner's interest on whether the arm had been deposited in the Coogee pool as a result of a student prank.

Months later, at the court proceedings against Brady, no further official thinking was advanced on the actual cause of Smith's death. The prosecution largely relied upon Brady's presence in the vicinity of Cored Joy as the foundation of its case, coupled with the opportunity to kill Smith he appeared to have been given.

Brady himself once referred to the possibility that Jim Smith had died from gunshot wounds, without saying who might have killed him. Late in his life, he told Sydney journalist Vince Kelly that information had been 'leaked' to his lawyers that one of the wounds on Smith's arm 'was done by a bullet'. He did not identify the source of this report. He then went on: 'I have never carried a lethal weapon in my life.'

Brady also cited his long-standing friendship with Smith as a reason he was hardly likely to have killed him. He said: 'I can truthfully say that Jim and I never had a difference about anything in the years of our friendship.' Even if this was an overstatement, its substance was confirmed by his wife. It was not incompatible with what the police knew of their relationship. Smith's banter with his mother-in-law on the morning he left home for the last time after being summoned to Cronulla by Brady's son did nothing to contradict it. Nor was there evidence that the friendship between the two men had broken down on the last occasion they had been seen together publicly at the Cecil.

Brady's only direct accuser was Reginald Holmes. In the one formal statement Holmes made, he claimed that Smith had told him he had been threatened by his long-time friend. Brady, however, always denied this. Many years later Brady affirmed that 'no one regretted more than my counsel and myself that Holmes didn't enter the witness box to be examined on his statements'. He went on: 'The public would have heard a fuller story . . .'

Brady claimed, too, that he would have been physically incapable of killing Smith. He pointed out that he was considerably shorter than the dead man, who was 'well built, and a former pugilist, and kept himself in good condition'. This did not absolve him from murder if he had acted in concert with others. But it helped to confirm the belief the detectives had formed early in their inquiries that, however Brady might have been involved, he was not alone in carrying out some of the acts they suspected had taken place at Cored Joy.

Some of the evidence presented against Brady was equally compatible with his claim that he had not killed Smith. His dishevelled condition and odd behaviour on the morning of 9 April could have been viewed as evidence that Brady was in a state of desperation, left to deal with a situation that was not of his own making.

But even if Brady did not kill Smith, he may still have been criminally liable in relation to his death. The evidence the police gathered about the forger's subsequent dealings with Reginald Holmes, and the testimony of Bert McGowan and others about his purchase of the trunk and the kapok mattress, point strongly to Brady's involvement in covering up the events the police believed had occurred in the vicinity of Cored Joy. In this he appears to have played a leading role, not least in forcing Holmes to assist by providing money, and perhaps in other ways.

Brady denied that he ever carried Smith's arm to McMahon's Point. Curiously, however, he never seems to have been precise about this. His one clear response to the claim in his discussions with Vince Kelly was in the form of a rhetorical question: 'Would I be so utterly stupid to carry it about with me, even briefly, a severed arm that would get anyone carrying it an indictment for murder?' He never explained what had happened to the heavy killick, the manilla rope and the anchor that had been attached to the motorboat he had hired and returned to the Smith family of Taloombi Street. He also never related what had happened to the brown leather kitbag he had carried back to Cronulla in Bert McGowan's taxi, or why he had taken it to Holmes's residence the night before.

But if Patrick Brady didn't kill Jim Smith, who did? The CIB seriously considered two alternative scenarios that never surfaced in official proceedings. One centred on the possibility that Reginald Holmes or some of his associates had killed Smith. The other had little to do with either the boatbuilder or the forger.

Chapter 30

A BOATBUILDER'S LEGACIES

Reginald William Lloyd Holmes left a variety of legacies. One was a family boatbuilding enterprise on the shoreline of Lavender Bay. Another was a large personal estate. But he also left his wife and two children under police guard for months after his murder, bereft of their breadwinner, surrounded by unwelcome publicity.

Like the Brady family, the Holmeses lived for many years in the shadow of uncertainty about the role the late boatbuilder might have played in Jim Smith's disappearance. As Patrick Brady said when interviewed by Vince Kelly in the early 1960s, there were people who had deep suspicions about Holmes's involvement. To Kelly: 'Reg Holmes was the one person whose evidence from the witness stand could have sent others to the gallows.' More than fifty years later, a former neighbour still remembered Holmes mostly because of the long-held belief that he had been involved in Jim Smith's murder.

The boatbuilder was not as pure as snow. Among some of his North Shore friends and neighbours his smuggling activities might have had a swashbuckling 'Boy's Own Paper' air about them. Essentially, however, he was a crook. He profited from illegal activities, was not afraid to use a pistol threateningly, and traded on his social position to protect himself. If he was vulnerable to blackmail, he had only himself to blame.

Holmes may have started to loathe Smith, even threaten him, after the financial debacle that followed the scuttling of the *Pathfinder* and after Smith's attempt to blackmail him. There was much evidence to this effect, coming from Inie Holmes, some of Holmes's employees and, if they were to be believed, the comments Holmes himself made on the *Nemesis*. But there was no evidence that he had killed the missing man and a good deal of evidence to the contrary.

The chief accuser alleging the boatbuilder's involvement in Smith's disappearance was Patrick Brady. But he never charged Holmes with actually killing Smith. In the forger's second statement to the police, he said that Holmes visited Cored Joy after Smith left on the night of 8 April, the night the police believed Smith died. Whether this was true or not, it was certainly no accusation of murder.

In Brady's remarks to Vince Kelly, he did not refer back to his earlier claim that Holmes had been at Cored Joy on the night of 8 April, and probably advisedly so. At the time he made the claim in his second statement, it was likely that he was using it to set up an alibi for himself, not seeking to protect Holmes.

The police had credible evidence that Holmes had not been in the vicinity of Cored Joy on that particular night. There were firm statements from Inie Holmes and a household servant that the boatbuilder had been at home from the early evening, and no indications from anyone else the police interviewed that this was untrue.

There were more doubts, however, about some of the boatbuilder's movements in the forty-eight hours after Brady arrived at McMahon's Point with taxi-driver Bill Brown. The police had little doubt that, after Brady's early morning visit, Holmes spent the rest of the day going about his normal pursuits. It was clear, too, that he arrived at home as usual before Brady returned later, carrying the brown kitbag. After that, there were gaps in the police knowledge about his movements that they were never able to fill.

The police were suspicious that, after Brady's night visit, Holmes drove off with him and was present when the tattooed arm was thrown into the sea at Maroubra, and then delivered Brady to where the forger's wife and son were staying not far away. To Detective Danny Calman, at least, the way Holmes seemed to know where the arm was thrown into the sea suggested he might well have witnessed the event.

This hypothesis gave a possible explanation why there were no records of Brady using taxis on the night of 9 April, when he used them so often otherwise. The police also found that Inie Holmes seemed more equivocal about whether her husband was home for the rest of the evening after Brady's visit, compared to her first affirmation that he was home the previous night.

Most of Holmes's movements on the day after Brady's night visit on 9 April seem to have been accounted for satisfactorily. The police considered him most likely to have been the person Brady was planning to meet when he set out in Bert McGowan's taxi in the morning, particularly as he was one of the very few of the forger's acquaintances known to have a private car. But, as Bert McGowan said, the person Brady was expecting never arrived. There were some gaps in the police knowledge of Holmes's activities later in the day. Brady seemed prepared to acknowledge that Smith was dead by then, however, even though he also claimed the missing man did not die the night before.

If Holmes did not kill Smith himself, as Brady seemed to accept, it seemed to Vince Kelly that he was perhaps the chief instigator, in association with others who actually carried out the murder. Brady went part way to inferring as much when he said that a friend of Holmes was one of the mysterious visitors to Cored Joy on the night of 8 April. These visitors, he said, took Smith away with them.

The police did not dismiss this possibility lightly, as their futile search for items Brady said had been left at Cored Joy by Holmes's associates demonstrated. They remained alert to it in their dealings with the boatbuilder. Despite this, they appear to have been unable to discover any credible evidence that Holmes or his associates engineered Smith's death.

The initial police reaction to Holmes's description of Brady producing the tattooed arm in his study was bemused disbelief. The scene appeared to be stimulated by fantasy brought on by the boatbuilder's mental condition. But as their questioning had gone on, they had become less sure, particularly in light of the information they had about the movements of the brown kitbag that Brady would not discuss.

For a time, detectives had contemplated a scenario that varied considerably from Holmes's versions of his meetings with Brady on 9 April. They entertained the notion that Brady had been acting on Holmes's behalf in arranging for Smith to be killed. At the first meeting after Brady's ride with Bill Brown, so the hypothesis ran, Brady had arrived at McMahon's

Point to inform the boatbuilder that Smith had been killed and to arrange for the fee to be paid. But Holmes had reneged, and Brady had returned that night with Smith's arm to force him to pay up.

There were good reasons why this theory was rejected. It assumed that Smith's body was still at Cored Joy when Brady set out to visit Holmes, and that the forger then returned to the cottage and cut off the arm, disposing of the rest of Smith's body later. It was far more likely, police agreed early in their inquiries, that the remainder of Smith's body was dumped in Gunnamatta Bay before Brady set out on his early morning taxi ride.

Additionally, police information indicated that, before Smith's death, the relationship between Brady and Holmes was based purely on a forgery enterprise. Matthews, Allmond and other officers who spoke with Holmes finally came to the conclusion that, however fanciful the story of the arm in the study might seem, the boatbuilder was probably telling the truth.

On the other hand, more than one of the group of detectives had lingering suspicions after Brady's acquittal that one or more of Holmes's associates had been responsible for Smith's death, whether the boatbuilder himself was directly responsible or not. It was a possibility that Patrick Brady hinted at late in his life. He claimed that one theory about Smith's murder was that he had been killed by the same person who had murdered Holmes, using the same gun.

In their investigations into the deaths of both Smith and Holmes, however, the detectives found no firm evidence to make this connection. A search for the weapon used to kill Holmes was futile. Careful checks on the movements of the men who had been associated with Smith and Holmes in the sinking of the *Pathfinder* and in smuggling activities also produced no evidence that any of them had been at Cronulla when Smith had been there.

In the records the police amassed on the deaths of Smith and Holmes, however, there were scattered reports suggesting that Brady and Holmes were not the only people who could be viewed with suspicion in the murder of Smith. These reports were not entirely ignored by the CIB in their inquiries. But they were largely put to one side as the police investigations centred on Brady and Holmes in the lead-up to the Coroner's inquiry into Jim Smith's death. Taken with other information the police had obtained, these reports suggested reasons for Smith's disappearance that were not advanced in the public hearings.

Chapter 31

MORNING IN SURRY HILLS

At the time of his arrest, Matthews and Allmond had already determined that it was highly unlikely that Patrick Brady had acted alone in the murder of Jim Smith and the disposal of his body. They confidently expected that, after a time, the forger would succumb to their pressure and reveal the true facts about Smith's disappearance. Brady said, many years later, that when Allmond had met him alone at Central Street on the night of his arrest, he had told Brady he could go free if he disclosed who had really killed Jim Smith. Allmond never seems to have denied this assertion, and there is no reason to disbelieve what Brady said.

At the time of Brady's interrogation the detectives appear to have had no certain ideas about the identities of other suspects. They were depending upon Brady to provide this information. Later, however, during the course of their further investigations, they obtained testimony from other sources, some on public record, suggesting that Smith's murder could well have nothing to do with Brady, Holmes, or any of the boatbuilder's associates.

For Brady, and perhaps others, the most potent reminder of who else might have been responsible for Smith's murder seems to have taken place almost ten years later. It came with the discovery of the body of a thirty-four-year-old man at dawn on New Year's Day, 1945. The corpse was found on concrete steps leading to the street from the basement of a house at Surry Hills, a suburb of Sydney on the fringe of Kings Cross. The body was clothed in only a blood-stained singlet. A trail of blood led to a bedroom where the man had been shot five times the night before.

The victim's name was Edward Frederick Weyman, commonly known as 'Eddie'. His murder had nothing to do with Smith's death. A decade before, however, he had been well acquainted with Patrick Brady. More significantly, he had not only known Jim Smith but had made repeated threats against his life.

Weyman was 'well known to the police', as the *Sydney Morning Herald* reported. The paper revealed that he 'had served several gaol terms, and was a convicted sly-grog seller'. A few days before his death, he had been involved in what the paper called a 'mystery shooting', and had been taken to a nearby hospital with a bullet in his left arm. His criminal record showed that he had been one of the more brutal members of Sydney's criminal fraternity.

In the mid-1930s Weyman was one of a coterie of criminals that treated Brady like a 'guru' who was able to dispense advice on dealings with the police and other matters. After Brady came out of gaol in December 1933, Weyman was seen more and more in his company in hotel bars, often with Jim Smith in attendance. It was precisely these sorts of connections that caused Sergeant Arantz of the Balmain police to inveigle Smith into becoming a police informer, and he was not disappointed.

In August 1934, with information supplied by Smith to the police, Weyman was caught attempting to defraud a bank. He pretended to be a messenger presenting a cheque to one of its tellers. The cheque was forged, as the police were fore-warned, and Weyman was caught red-handed. An older accomplice, surnamed Cottenham, was arrested soon after. Cottenham was sent to gaol. For Weyman it was his first conviction for a serious criminal offence, and he was allowed to remain free on a bond.

In the normal course this might not have mattered to Smith. The police, in their usual way, covered up the source of the information that led to these convictions. Despite this, both Cottenham and Weyman claimed volubly that Smith had 'shelved' them to the police.

Weyman was not mentioned by name in the court proceedings on Jim Smith's disappearance. He did not feature prominently in the police records relating to it. Patrick Brady, however, had not forgotten him when interviewed by Vince Kelly. He linked Weyman centrally to the circumstances surrounding the disappearance. He contended that the aborted bank robbery could not be ignored. He remarked: 'This episode must be kept in mind for its repercussions of alleged blackmail and murder threats in the Shark Arm Case.'

Weyman was one of several men Allmond and other detectives had in mind as possible suspects by the time of the Coroner's inquiry into Smith's death. If Smith was killed with a pistol, Weyman was a far more likely suspect than Brady, who was never known to use firearms. Above all, in further contrast to Brady, there was strongly corroborated testimony that Weyman had threatened Smith.

One of the chief weaknesses of the case against Brady

was the prosecution's failure to ascribe to him any strong motive for killing Jim Smith. The only suggestion that Brady had fallen out with Smith came from Reginald Holmes. As the boatbuilder told the police, Smith once told him he was being threatened by 'Brady and his friend' and that 'they blame me [Smith] for putting the cops on them over a cheque'. Countervailing this, however, was an abundance of testimony from Grace Brady, Gladys Smith and others that the friendship between the two men had not broken down.

The situation was far different in the case of the 'friend' Holmes had referred to. It had not taken the police long to discover that this was Eddie Weyman. Soon, there was an array of evidence that this hood had not only verbally threatened Smith but, on one occasion at least, had threatened him with a gun.

As Gladys Smith described one incident, Weyman had burst unannounced into her Gladesville home demanding money from her husband. He shouted out that he blamed Smith for his recent arrest. Gladys recalled that Weyman had pulled a pistol from one of his pockets when Smith remonstrated with him. 'I ought to blow your guts out,' she remembered him saying, as he pointed the pistol at her husband's stomach. Smith had finally placated the unwelcome visitor by promising to give him money he said Reginald Holmes owed him.

Gladys and other members of her family also claimed this was not the only time Weyman had threatened Jim Smith's life. She told the police that she had feared also for her own and her family's lives. She had nervously accompanied her husband on a visit to Holmes to beg the boatbuilder to give them money for Weyman.

Unlike with Brady, the CIB was unable to find evidence that Weyman was in the vicinity of Cored Joy when Smith disappeared. Jim Smith, the chief police informant about his activities, was dead. Brady was not likely to change his habits of a lifetime and dob in a mate, however this might serve his interests. Weyman's growing reputation for violence made it difficult to cajole fizgigs to provide information about him.

Many years later, however, the possibility that Weyman could have been a visitor to Cored Joy was revealed by Grace Brady. Smith, it seems, was not the only one of Brady's friends who visited him at Cored Joy. Grace recalled that she had become uncharacteristically suspicious of her husband during his lengthy stay at Cored Joy, thinking he might have been cheating on her with another woman. She had made her way stealthily to Taloombi Street at night, and crept down the wooden steps to the cottage. Through a window she saw Brady playing cards with other men, with bottles of beer and half-filled glasses scattered around. She left as unobtrusively as she had arrived, relieved by what she had seen.

If Weyman was a visitor to the waterfront cottage when Smith was there, much of the evidence presented against Brady could have been construed far differently. Rather than being used in a bid to implicate him directly in Jim Smith's murder, it could have been taken to point to Weyman as its perpetrator. It might also have made it possible to give a more satisfactory official explanation of why the tattooed arm had been severed from the dead man's body.

Patrick Brady's love of fishing was no affectation, as Percival Forbes, the owner of Cored Joy had found. The night of 8–9 April 1935, as official records show, was a good time to fish in Port Hacking. If Brady spoke truthfully on 9 April in his meetings with Bill Brown and others, he had spent most of the night engaged in this pastime. If this was so, it was quite possible he was not even present at Cored Joy when Smith died. Instead, someone like Weyman could have been at the cottage in the interim, killing Smith while Brady was away.

If this or something like it was the true course of events Brady could well have been far more a victim of circumstance than the official case against him ever revealed. Feasibly, his dishevelled appearance, and his seemingly distraught state on the morning of 9 April, could have resulted from shock after returning to Cored Joy to find Smith murdered – with Brady left to remove traces of Smith's disappearance from the waterfront cottage, clearly uncertain of where he might turn for help, as he revealed on his journey to North Sydney with Bill Brown.

As he journeyed to Sydney, Brady seemed to show signs of fear, glancing apprehensively through the rear window of Bill Brown's taxi, carefully pulling down a side blind, as if frightened he was being followed. This may well have been so if Weyman was the person who had killed Jim Smith. Brady might have been in fear for his life, knowing of Weyman's violent disposition, realising that Weyman would seek to eliminate him as a knowledgeable witness of what had occurred at the waterfront cottage.

Unlike Brady, Weyman seemed the type capable of deliberately severing Jim Smith's arm from the remainder of his body, if this is what happened. It was not beyond him, as his lack of respect for human life demonstrated later, to have cut the arm off as a macabre warning to Brady when he returned from fishing. Weyman, assisted by a confederate, may have meanwhile disposed of the rest of Smith's body and left Cored Joy before Brady got back, leaving just the arm.

Like so much else surrounding Jim Smith's death and the disposal of his body, the possibility that Eddie Weyman was Jim Smith's murderer can only be conjectured. The position could well be otherwise, however, if the remainder of Smith's body is ever found in Percival Forbes's metal container, probably still resting on the floor of Port Hacking. If this discovery reveals that Smith died from gunshot wounds, Weyman will be confirmed as the most likely person to have actually killed Jim Smith, almost certainly with a companion who helped him dispose of Smith's body, except his tattooed arm, on the night of 8 April 1935.

Failing this, in the style of Scots law, Weyman's guilt can only be recorded as 'not proven'. Such a verdict, as Scottish law has long provided, means that it simply cannot be proved beyond reasonable doubt, as the law requires, that Weyman was the person who murdered Smith. At the same time, as Scots law also acknowledges in these circumstances, there is a good chance that he did.

Above: The Coogee
Aquarium where the
Tiger shark disgorged
the tattooed arm of
Jim Smith.
Right: The shark in
Coogee Aquarium,
April 1935.

HOLMES MURDER CUNNINGLY PLANNED
TRAIN MUFFLED SHOTS
Killer Took His Victim to Dark And Lonely Spot

WAS WITNESS AT SMITH CASE

MUFFLED by the roar of a train over head, three shots were fired in a car in Hickson-road, Dawes Point, last night, and Reginald William Holmes, famous boatbuilder, slumped over the wheel, murdered; and another chapter was added to one of the most dramatic stories in the history of Australia.

HOLMES was to have been one of the principal witnesses in the tattooed arm inquiry by the Coroner to-day and his death sets C.I.B. detectives a new problem in that already sensational and perplexing mystery, which followed the finding of a human arm beside a shark in the Coogee Aquarium Baths on Anzac Day.

THREE shells, of .32 calibre bullets, were found in the car, two of them on the front seat near the body and the third on the back seat. The left-hand door of the car—a sedan—had been left open, presumably by the murderer before making his dash into the midnight quiet of one of the loneliest and least frequented parts of the city's waterfront. No resolve was found.

Eerie Scene At Car In The Dawn

Gangster Fashion

THE SUN STOP-PRESS

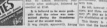

In Train's Roar

POLICE TASK
Tracing Movements

Faces Mystery

The Post Mortem

IN CHALK
Preserve Prints
ON CAR

TO END DAYS
In Isolation
MEN ON ISLAND

AUCKLAND, Wednesday.

SUPREME
HOLMES'S BOATS
SKILFUL WORK
BUILT PEARLERS

Preferred Background

Piercing Rays Probe Darkness For Clues

Exciting Chase

61 Years Married

Right: Jim Smith, the missing man.
Below: C. Hobson (left), the owner of the Coogee Aquarium when the shark was caught by his brother, B. Hobson (right).
Left: Front page of the *Sun* showing the Coroner's findings at the time of the inquest.

THE SUN

LATE FINAL EXTRA

FOR AUSTRALIA

TATTOOED ARM WAS CUT WITH KNIFE

DOCTOR'S EVIDENCE

Not Severed By Bite From Shark

ROPE HITCH ON WRIST

Crowd Watches Demonstration In Court

Rajpolf William Holmes, who was the deaf in his care ns to Hilsen and, Davis Point, yesterday morning. He was widely known as an expert footballer. His photograph was taken some time ago.

EVIDENCE that the tattooed arm found in the Coogee Aquarium on Anzac Day had been cut from a body that probably was already dead, and that disarticulation had not been done by a surgeon, was given by the Government Medical Officer, Dr. Palmer, at the resumed inquest to-day into the death of James Smith.

"I can say definitely that it was not severed by a shark bite but by a sharp knife," said Dr. Palmer. "I cannot say, though, how long the arm had been removed from the body, because I do not know any single reason why an arm should remain in a shark for a week or more without any appearance of digestion showing in the arm. Tests made showed that the person from whom the arm was taken had not died from poison."

An old rope, like a kellick rope, was around the wrist, tied in a clove-hitch, said Dr. Palmer. The crowd in the Court craned forward as, in a casual manner, he tied a rope on his own wrist and demonstrated how the ends of the rope hung away from the arm.

PEACE AIM

CALL FOR CRUSADE

Non-Party Manifesto

ELECTION POINTS

("Sun" Special)

LONDON, Wednesday.

MR. LLOYD GEORGE, leader of the Free Churches and others, to-day issued a non-party manifesto urging the institution of a fresh crusade for peace and national reconstruction.

The manifesto states that the approaching election may return the most fateful Parliament in British history and therefore citizens must ensure that its membership will accomplish a courageous grappling with vital issues.

The failure of successive Parliaments to deal adequately with world and economic problems had caused anxious and despair that constituted a national danger.

All resources must be mobilised to avert irreparable disaster and to ensure that peoples of the world took an infinite passion for peace and social service.

Injustices Which Breed War

The election should support any candidate pledged to building up Britain's facilities to redress the injustices which bred war and also pledged to practical disarmament, the maintenance of peace through the League of Nations, a supreme...

Mr Lloyd George today

... effort towards international reconciliation, a League agreement for the abolition of offensive war instruments; a reduction of arms to police level control of the private manufacture of armaments; a public control of the abolition of the tariffs and the positive guarantee of collective guarantees.

A convention will be held on July 1 to create a "council for peace and reconstruction."

The Signatories

The signatories included Mrs Corbett-Ashby admitting delegate to the United Kingdom to the Disarmament Conference; the Bishop of Birmingham; Dr Barnes; Mr E A J Fisher Warden of New College Oxford; Mr Lionel George; Sir Walter Layton, editor of the "Economist"; Rev Scott Lidgett, Methodist of the "Contemporary Review," and first president of the United Methodist Church; Lord Lothian, secretary of the Rhodes Trust; Mr Gilbert Murray, Regius Professor of Greek at Oxford University; Rev F W Norwood of the City Temple; Mr Seebohm Rowntree, editor of "The Christian World" and Lord Snowden.

F. PERRY—DIRECTOR

A NEW JOB

Sporting Firm

ANOTHER TOUR

("Sun" Special)

LONDON, Wednesday.

GREAT BRITAIN'S No. 1 tennis player, Fred Perry, will, it is stated, join the sporting firm of Slazengers as a director.

In that capacity he is understood to have Australia at the end of the tennis here and compete in the major tournaments.

McGRATH IN FORM

DAVIS CUP DRAW

(From Harry Hopman)

BERLIN, Wednesday.

A capacity gate is likely on the first and third days of the Davis Cup match between Germany and Australia, the gallery declining on the second day owing to the impression that the Australians will win the doubles.

The Australians, practising below-screen, put only a glimpse of form, McGrath again being unleashed.

The Germans are resting. Norman Brookes played to a practise doubles with many pre-war top successor companions who visited the club to create arrangements.

The draw for the match is—Friday: Display J. Crawford v. von Cramm; V. B. McGrath v. H. Henkel.

Saturday — Doubles — Presents Lester Crawford and Quist v. von Cramm and R. Goebler.

Monday—McGrath v. von Cramm; Crawford v. Henkel.

CANADIAN WHEAT POOLS

Ottawa, Wednesday—The Prime Minister, Mr Bennett, stated in Parliament to-day that the selling agency of the Canadian Pools had sold 30,000,000 bushels for the release of Charles Churcul Pool Elevators in this crew at fifty cents a bushel...

FOR KING

PRINCE AS DEPUTY

KING'S ILLNESS

JUBILEE EVENTS

("Sun" Special)

LONDON, Wednesday.

THE Prince of Wales will deputise for the King at some of the remaining Jubilee functions, while the latter takes two weeks' complete rest, consequent upon his internal catarrh.

The Queen returned to Buckingham Palace this afternoon from Sandringham, where the King was well enough to accompany an hour's motor drive.

The King's doctors are confident that the fresh air of Windsor and rest will soon enable the King to throw off the effects of the attack.

Engagements which the King has been compelled to cancel include a visit to the opera to-night, where the American prima donna, Grace Moore, is appearing in "La Boheme," and the Court ball to-morrow.

At the ball the Prince will lead the Queen into the state and pink ballroom at Buckingham Palace in place of the King.

The Queen will take up residence at Windsor Castle on Saturday.

KIDNAP FEES

Lawyers Accused

("Sun" Special)

NEW YORK, Wednesday.

THE Federal authorities are trying not only to eliminate kidnapping, but to "make it hot" for the lawyers who defend them.

Two Oklahoma attorneys, Leslie and Malcom are charged with participation in accepting £300 to free, knowing that the money was portion of 240,000 which Harvey Bailey and "Machine Gun" Kelly obtained for the release of Charles Urschel.

Five kidnappers in this case already have been sentenced to life imprisonment.

THE SUN STOP-PRESS

DOCTOR'S DEATH

Dr F M O'Donnell, woollen-mills doctor, was also well-known. Holmes died in the St Canice Parish Hall.

Internal continued unflagged when the inquest was resumed and crowds again jostled to get positions.

Patrick Brady, who has been charged with the murder of Smith, was present in custody.

When the court resumed, Sergeant Toole handed to Mr Evatt a stave sword with broke blade found on the body. There was some bone which was protruded received by Mrs Keith Thom, he said. Mr Evatt had requested successive...

Recalled to the witness-box, Mrs Gladys Lillian Jane Steward Smith, wife of James Smith, said that at 3.30-p.m. standing at the Club door a fair show of hats bases by Dr Palmer.

Medical Officer. The finch had been...

removed from the arm that had been found in the Coogee Aquarium.

Before she had been shown this piece of flesh she had expected a month apply hooked to get positions.

When she was shown, Sergeant Toole handed to Mr Evatt a stave sword with broke blade... on his arm... protruding the bones to a crushing position... to the wrist... and back with red breaks.

On the ends of the pieces of flesh shown by the doctor was a peculiar design tattooed.

Medical Officer. The finch had been...

"I am sure that they are the marks..."

Found No Sign Of Poison In Arm

DR Arthur Aubrey Palmer (Government Medical Officer) says that on April 30 he examined a left upper limb identified to him by Constable Meillon as having been brought from an aquarium and said to have been severed by a shark. He expressed no opinion of how it was severed.

There had been disarticulation at the shoulder-joint, where the skin had been cut by a sharp knife, continued Dr Palmer.

The head of the arm bone was normal in cartilage which showed numerous abrasions and a mark wore out which had been attempted.

Other Cables on Page 2.

... escaped by a sharp instrument. There was a number of small abrasions' wounds on the arm and a big wound above the elbow, also caused by a sharp knife.

On the forearm there was a tattoo mark of two boxers facing as it when outlined to dark blue with red trunks.

The limb was in a good state of preservation, although it had decomposed slightly.

Dr Palmer said he had communicated with Dr Coppleson, of Macquarie-street, who had written about shark marked sharks and shark bites together they made an external examination of the arm.

"Not Work Of Shark"

Dr Palmer said that he had made a partial dissection of the arm and examined the marks to see if there had been any injection of preservatives, but he could find none. He had also subscribed the bulk of the tissue to the Government Analyst, whose report he produced to the Coroner.

On this report and on his own observations he said certainly that he was not an anatomical specimen, nor had it been preserved by a corpse, as there were no flaps of skin to cover the wound.

"If the person from whom the arm came had died from preserving these would almost certainly have been some traces of the poison in the muscles but I could find no such trace," declared Dr Palmer.

Asked by the Coroner if the arm could have been removed from the body to a shark side Dr Palmer said he was firmly convinced that it made no have been.

He was also of the opinion that the arm had been removed from a dead body because there was no blood in the arms.

Both of the entire arms on this page so as produced appearing in "The Times," and is added to "The Sun" by medical permission. It should be understood that his opinion given are not those of "The Times" whose expressly stated to be so.

... Both of blood into the tissues around the cut.

He could not say how long it had been removed from the body "If the arm had been in a shark for a week," said Dr Palmer, "I know of no reason why it should not have been digested as I have conferred with University professors, and one of them suggested that a possible reason may have been that a shark in captivity is generally a frightened animal and that the gastric secretions may have been inhibited by fear in its strange surroundings."

Dr Coppleson also suggested that a shark finds great difficulty in digesting human flesh."

Further questioned by the Coroner Dr Palmer said that, although it was a wonderful coincidence, it was quite possible that the arm had been swallowed by a shark, which in turn had been swallowed by another shark, and that the arm had remained in the second shark after the first shark had been digested.

... sought had swallowed the arm and then slung onto the hip they shark and into the air. Digestion would commence with the swallowing fish and until that kept up the digestion of the arm would not commence.

"I do not know whether the arm had reached the shark's stomach at all," he added. "My job is with human anatomy and I do not know that of a shark."

Mr Evatt: It was a million-to-one chance that digestion would not have taken place in the shark?—Yes.

That is it was a million-to-one chance that this one shark in all the sea should have been the only one to be the only one to be thrown into the sea alive.

Assuming that there was no evidence that the arm was sought you are confine to the theory that this arm was not digested?—I would be inclined to think that.

Mr Evatt said that in view of Dr Palmer's evidence and suggestions he thought the time was appropriate.

Unfinished Work At Boatshed

Launches under construction at the boatshed at McMahon's Point, at the time of the ex-owner Rajpolf William Holmes.

Dr Palmer said he could not state any suggestion as to how the arm came off. But the ends that had been found showing a loose tissue and raw sheets which normally have shown signs of decomposing if the arm think that the arms would have fitted as it appeared to this the arm was unquestionably undergoing to an immaculate person, and the error therefore would probably have lead to death.

Cross-examined by Mr Evatt Dr Palmer admitted that the only thing which made him certain the arm had come from a dead body was that there was no blood in the arm. It was conceivably conceivable although it was his opinion that it had come from a dead body.

Get Own Doctor

One theory said Dr Palmer that the first shark on the one which the Coogee shark had been...

Only Skin Left

The Coroner (Mr Oram) said that anything that would help in the inquiry would be allowed. Unfortunately there already so very little of the arm to examine properly. All that was left was the skin, rather cosily noting an explained matter it had no attention to any medical man who wanted to examine the matter.

Dr Palmer said that most of the arm had been put up to the Analyst and practically all that was left, the fashioned skin.

(Continued on Page 22)

Crazy Air Acrobat Has Nerve To Talk

("Sun" Special)

LONDON, Thursday.

THIS year's Royal Air Force display, to be held at Hendon on June 29, will contain one novel feature.

This will be a description broadcast by a pilot engaged in acrobatic flying.

With a microphone attached to his head, he will describe every movement he makes.

This will be done even when he is flying upside-down, when he deliberately stalls his machine and when in a driving nose-dive in the north at all-direction demolished speed.

He will also explain what he does to prevent from these dangerous and unorthodox positions.

By internal arrangement, Reuter's World Service, in addition to other special services of information, is solely responsible for all matter appearing in "The Sun" and all rights thereto is placed with "The Sun." Copyright in Great Britain and New Zealand are reserved.

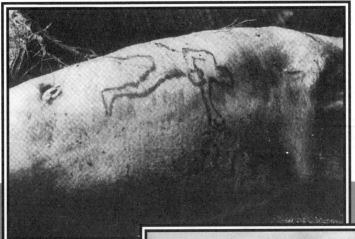

Above: The tattooed arm of Jim Smith, disgorged by a captured Tiger shark.
Right: Detective-Sergeant Frank Matthews, later Superintendent and chief of the Sydney CIB.
Left: The front page of the *Sun* on the second day of the coronial inquest.

16 May 1935

1 I have been D'in connection of a man named
2 James Smith & am making this statement
3 & is in which I will explain movements
4 so far as I can remember
5 I have known James Smith for 30 years, he was
6 a local resident of Rozelle.
7 I was in Tasmania and left there about the 9th
8 March and on arrival I stayed at 2 Liddle St
9 One day shortly I received a telephone message
10 at 24 Gladstone Rd from Smith come in
11 consequence I went to his home at 14 Pelican Rd
12 Gladesville.
13 In the course of talk a discussion came up
14 about a cheque which was to he use, saying
15 he would arrange with Mr Holmes to get the
16 materials, Holmes I knew about a month.
17 I first met him at Bayview Rd and was introduced
18 to him by James Smith, who was looking
19 after a boat called the Pathfinder problem
20 & that.
21 On the 30th March I had a cottage boxed up at Cronulla
22 and later occupied it with my wife and
23 then the only visitors I had were my relations
24 of Brampton, his family, my Mother in law &
25 single ones of the day time. They only coming at
26 week ends I took possession on the 30 March.
27 I hired a launch from a man named Jim Hill
28 and used it occasionally. it was used by
29 me mostly week ends. It was to be used by
30 the owner if he wanted it.
31 I stayed out there till the 31st of April but
32 had a right to to stay till the 17th
33 James Smith was there on the previous
34 and the last time I left him was at on the
35 9th of April at Cronulla. I went into town

Right: Boatbuilder Reginald Holmes, the murdered star witness.
Below: Cored Joy, the holiday cottage rented by Brady.

Left: Desolate area around Dawes Point where Holmes's dead body was found.
Below: The plaque on the Sydney Coroners Court.
Bottom: The site of the Coogee Aquarium.

CITY CORONERS COURT 1907

The City Morgue was built on the eastern part of this site in 1906. The City Coroners Court, designed by the Government Architect in the Edwardian style, was completed in 1908 for the sum of £4258 by J. J. Turner, Builder, of Waverley. Many famous Coroners Enquiries were held here, the best known being the Shark Arm Case in 1935, in which a missing criminal was identified by a tattoo on an arm found in a shark's stomach.

EPILOGUE

After 1935, the people involved in the shark arm inquiries went their separate ways. The traumatic events continued to haunt some of them, in particular Patrick Brady, as newspapers, magazines and later television continued to revive public interest in the murders, too often relying on imagination rather than facts.

William Prior retired from his post in the Sydney CIB after a lifetime of service in the New South Wales police. From humble beginnings in a remote country district, he had enjoyed an astoundingly successful career. The reciprocal respect between the Superintendent and Brady was hardly an accident. Both were men from working-class Australian backgrounds, who shared some common ideas about fairness.

Time vindicated the Superintendent's early belief that the tattooed arm was already in the Tiger shark when it arrived at the Coogee pool. Scientific research has since confirmed that Tiger sharks have a peculiar dietary habit that probably goes back to before the age of dinosaurs. In a random fashion they can retain food in their stomachs, more or less in its original condition, for weeks and even months. Australian researchers have found the bodies of small dolphins and other marine animals intact in the intestines of Tiger sharks two months after they were swallowed. The best explanation seems to be that Tiger sharks have developed a capacity to maintain adequate supplies of food for times when it is scarce.

Of the other officers involved in the shark arm investigations, Frank Matthews later became a superintendent in charge of the Sydney CIB. Leonard Allmond, the more able of the two detective-sergeants in charge of the inquiries, left the CIB and returned to the uniformed branch of the police service when he was appointed as an inspector. Even after his retirement, Allmond was reluctant to say what he really thought of Matthews. He did acknowledge that he believed the inquiries into the deaths of Smith and Holmes had left his former colleague with some regrets, particularly about the death of the former North Sydney boatbuilder. Milner 'Danny' Calman, the most astute of the other detectives involved, also later rose through the ranks of the New South Wales police to head the Sydney CIB. He operated in the tradition of a detective force that was not renowned for brutality, in marked contrast to more than one other Australian law enforcement agency at that time.

Patrick Brady lived on to a good age, still happily married to Grace. Their only son, John, whom they called Jack, was killed serving the RAAF in a bombing raid over Germany in 1944. Brady told Vince Kelly, one of the best Sydney crime reporters ever, that the disappearance of Jim Smith scarred him for the rest of his life. He blamed the notoriety of the case for landing him in gaol for three years in Tasmania from 1938, after he was tried for the same forgery offence for the third time. He resented an American television program shown in Australia later that, he believed, was grossly unfair in its treatment of him. One Sydney newspaper announced his death, in August 1965, aged seventy-one, with a large headline and a story, and a photograph that covered the rest of the front page. It was coverage more normally reserved for the death of a prime minister.

Two people who were involved with the police investigations later died tragically. Inie Holmes was found dead at her home in October 1952. Her bedding and clothes had been burned after a fire caused by a cigarette. The finding of a coroner was that she had died from her burns. Gregory Vaughan, who had been the 'dummy' owner of the *Pathfinder*, committed suicide in a rooming house of Kings Cross in January 1940. His suicide note said: 'I have now taken twenty-eight didial tablets.' A coroner determined that his death had been caused by drugs that had been deliberately self-administered. Evidence was presented that the former real estate agent had been taking quantities of narcotics for several years.

After the body of Eddie Weyman was found, a well-known Sydney identity, 'Chow' Hayes, was charged with his murder and acquitted. Hayes collaborated with author David Hickie in a book published in 1990 that described him as 'Australia's most notorious gangster'. Hayes admitted in the book: 'I fired and hit him [Weyman] five times.' He added: 'The last I saw of him he fell down alongside the bed. I knew he was badly wounded and I thought he was dead – but he wasn't.' Hayes had then left Weyman's lodgings by the front door and had put his 'handkerchief over the knob so as not to leave fingerprints'. Mortally wounded, Weyman had managed only to crawl to his front door and open it.

Albert Stannard was unfortunately shadowed by the stigma of his trials for Reginald Holmes's murder. The evidence against him was slim. But for reasons the police never explained, he was charged, along with Jack Strong, for murder, even though the police had information suggesting that others could have committed the crime.

In the years since 1935 some of the landmarks that featured in the investigations have disappeared. The old Holmes boatshed on Lavender Bay has gone. The Cecil hotel at Cronulla has been replaced by a block of modern apartments. But the shell of its portico has been retained as part of the building, a memento of the days when the hotel was one of the district's most popular venues. The steam trains that once linked Cronulla with the rail service at Sutherland have also long since disappeared, replaced by a direct rail connection to central Sydney. Some of the old centres of waterfront intrigue around Circular Quay have also gone, victims of the alterations that have progressively taken place in the area since the second world war.

The building on Dolphin Street at Coogee where the tattooed arm appeared has also changed. The dome on its roof was retained, and preserved from rust. The building was later gaudily re-decorated outside, like an entertainment centre in Singapore or Hong Kong, with a large sign proclaiming it to be the Coogee Palace. Inside, the building was brightly lit. The swimming baths, with their mock Roman interior, have disappeared. But a plaque marks their passing and commemorates the strange events of Anzac Day, 1935.

Elsewhere, on George Street North, just up from Circular Quay, the building that once housed the Coroner's Court has a plaque on the wall outside recording the 'Shark Arm

Case' as the most notable hearing ever convened there. In the surrounding neighbourhood The Rocks has been upgraded as a tourist attraction, and the building is now used as a site to provide information about an area which was for years as tumultuous as New York's 'Hell's Kitchen'.

At Cronulla, the urban sprawl of the years after the second world war has overwhelmed Taloombi Street. Only a few older buildings remain. The bushland setting has gone, and the area has become typical of middle-class suburbia.

Like other Australian capital cities, Sydney has retained a blend of old and new. The Hickson Steps, near where Reginald Holmes was shot, are much as they were in 1935. At the top of the cliff, the same rooms in a tenement-lined street still look over the place where the boatbuilder's body was found in his Nash sedan. The wharves are still there, beside Walsh Bay, although they have been put to new uses. Reminders of the vehicular ferry terminals can be found where Hickson Road runs under the harbour bridge at Dawes Point. At Batemans Road in Gladesville, the Smith home also long remained much as it was when Jim Smith lived there.

Lower Bay View Street, McMahon's Point, is still a haven of genteel living, a short ferry ride from Circular Quay to reach the same wharf depicted so affectionately by Arthur Streeton in his famous painting of this location early in the twentieth century. The wharves around Long Nose Point, Balmain, have changed little, if at all, since Jim Smith met Sergeant Arantz there in 1934.

Since the second world war, police investigations in New South Wales, as elsewhere, have changed dramatically in nature. The CIB has long since moved from the building on Central Street to more commodious premises. New scientific aids and advances in forensic medicine have provided far more effective methods for detecting and proving the commission of crimes like the murders of Jim Smith and Reginald Holmes. At the same time, compared to the situation in 1935, when Patrick Brady was unceremoniously bundled away from North Sydney and subjected to relentless mental pressure for more than two days, new and fairer rules now govern law enforcement agencies in their dealings with suspects.

With all these changes, the effectiveness and fairness of a system of law enforcement still depends on the calibre and integrity of people charged with upholding it. If they are corrupted by outside influences, such as pressure from other parts of government, this system is jeopardised. Superintendent Prior and his colleagues did bend the law at times, but only in a context in which this was condoned by the local judicial system, following long-established English precedent. They were not involved in the systemic, institutionalised corruption with which the New South Wales police has sometimes been charged. They helped to demonstrate that, whatever its weaknesses, law enforcement can be carried on with reasonable integrity and fairness, to the benefit of the community it is called upon to serve.

A NOTE ON SOURCES

Had this book been an academic tome it would have been annotated with hundreds of footnotes. The narrative is based on a variety of primary source materials. These include, most importantly, the remaining transcripts of the official court proceedings into the disappearance of Jim Smith and the murder of Reginald Holmes. Where these could not be found, I used reports in contemporary newspapers to supplement them, mostly from the *Sydney Morning Herald*, occasionally from the *Sun*, *Labor Daily* and *Truth*. I read primary evidence of the police activities relating to both cases in the files retained in the archives of the New South Wales police. Some brief quotations from Patrick Brady and his wife, Grace, are taken from interviews carried out by Sydney journalist Vince Kelly in the early 1960s. These interviews were later published in part in the *Sun*, and formed the basis of the book *The Shark Arm Case* (1963), written by Kelly. The two quotations from 'Chow' Hayes are from his reminiscences as related to David Hickie in *Chow Hayes Gunman, Australia's Most Notorious Gangster* (1990).

    Some other material is taken from records of interviews I carried out myself. The most important were those with two of the detectives involved in the police investigations, Leonard Allmond and Milner 'Danny' Calman. Other interviews were with Sydney journalists who covered the cases for their newspapers. The most extensive and fruitful were with Syd King and Vince Kelly, ace crime reporters of the period. Kelly in particular had an encyclopaedic knowledge of the criminal milieu in Sydney as he evidenced in such books as *The Shadow* (1954), *The Bogey Man* (1956) and *The Rugged Angel* (1961).

From time to time I have also been given information by people who have preferred to remain anonymous. These sources have told me about the personal characters and family relationships of individuals who were involved in both cases. I have only used this information when it relates directly and significantly to the events portrayed. Otherwise, I have sought to protect family memories and, in some cases, present-day relationships.